RUSSIA: COUNTERTERRORISM PARTNER OR FANNING THE FLAMES?

JOINT HEARING

BEFORE THE

SUBCOMMITTEE ON TERRORISM, NONPROLIFERATION, AND TRADE

AND THE

SUBCOMMITTEE ON EUROPE, EURASIA, AND EMERGING THREATS

OF THE

COMMITTEE ON FOREIGN AFFAIRS HOUSE OF REPRESENTATIVES

ONE HUNDRED FIFTEENTH CONGRESS

FIRST SESSION

———

NOVEMBER 7, 2017

———

Serial No. 115–75

———

Printed for the use of the Committee on Foreign Affairs

Available via the World Wide Web: http://www.foreignaffairs.house.gov/ or
http://www.gpo.gov/fdsys/

———

U.S. GOVERNMENT PUBLISHING OFFICE

27–512PDF   WASHINGTON : 2017

For sale by the Superintendent of Documents, U.S. Government Publishing Office
Internet: bookstore.gpo.gov   Phone: toll free (866) 512–1800; DC area (202) 512–1800
Fax: (202) 512–2104   Mail: Stop IDCC, Washington, DC 20402–0001

COMMITTEE ON FOREIGN AFFAIRS

EDWARD R. ROYCE, California, *Chairman*

CHRISTOPHER H. SMITH, New Jersey
ILEANA ROS-LEHTINEN, Florida
DANA ROHRABACHER, California
STEVE CHABOT, Ohio
JOE WILSON, South Carolina
MICHAEL T. McCAUL, Texas
TED POE, Texas
DARRELL E. ISSA, California
TOM MARINO, Pennsylvania
MO BROOKS, Alabama PAUL
COOK, California SCOTT
PERRY, Pennsylvania RON
DeSANTIS, Florida
MARK MEADOWS, North Carolina
TED S. YOHO, Florida
ADAM KINZINGER, Illinois
LEE M. ZELDIN, New York
DANIEL M. DONOVAN, JR., New York
F. JAMES SENSENBRENNER, JR.,
  Wisconsin
ANN WAGNER, Missouri
BRIAN J. MAST, Florida
FRANCIS ROONEY, Florida
BRIAN K. FITZPATRICK, Pennsylvania
THOMAS A. GARRETT, JR., Virginia
Vacant

ELIOT L. ENGEL, New York
BRAD SHERMAN, California
GREGORY W. MEEKS, New York
ALBIO SIRES, New Jersey
GERALD E. CONNOLLY, Virginia
THEODORE E. DEUTCH, Florida
KAREN BASS, California
WILLIAM R. KEATING, Massachusetts
DAVID N. CICILLINE, Rhode Island
AMI BERA, California
LOIS FRANKEL, Florida
TULSI GABBARD, Hawaii
JOAQUIN CASTRO, Texas
ROBIN L. KELLY, Illinois
BRENDAN F. BOYLE, Pennsylvania
DINA TITUS, Nevada
NORMA J. TORRES, California
BRADLEY SCOTT SCHNEIDER, Illinois
THOMAS R. SUOZZI, New York
ADRIANO ESPAILLAT, New York
TED LIEU, California

AMY PORTER, *Chief of Staff*   THOMAS SHEEHY, *Staff Director*
JASON STEINBAUM, *Democratic Staff Director*

CONTENTS

Page

WITNESSES

LETTERS, STATEMENTS, ETC., SUBMITTED FOR THE HEARING

APPENDIX

RUSSIA: COUNTERTERRORISM PARTNER OR FANNING THE FLAMES?

TUESDAY, NOVEMBER 7, 2017

HOUSE OF REPRESENTATIVES,
SUBCOMMITTEE ON TERRORISM, NONPROLIFERATION, AND TRADE
AND
SUBCOMMITTEE ON EUROPE, EURASIA, AND EMERGING THREATS,
COMMITTEE ON FOREIGN AFFAIRS,
Washington, DC.

The subcommittees met, pursuant to notice, at 2:16 p.m., in room 2172, Rayburn House Office Building, Hon. Ted Poe (chairman of the Subcommittee on Terrorism, Nonproliferation, and Trade) presiding.

Mr. POE. The subcommittees will come to order. Without objection, all members may have 5 days to submit statements, questions, and extraneous materials for the record, subject to the length limitation in the rules. I will now recognize myself for 5 minutes in my opening statement.

The purpose of this hearing is to unmask Putin's two-faced game in the fight against terrorism. In 2015, Russia began a military intervention in Syria claiming it was waging war on ISIS and international terrorism.

To some, this was welcome news. It seemed that there may be a rare moment of cooperation between former Cold War foes. Moscow and Washington would be able to work together to combat terrorism.

This was fantasy. Moscow's actions in Syria has shown it is more interested in saving the brutal Assad regime than fighting ISIS.

To accomplish this goal, the Kremlin partnered with Iran and its terrorist proxies to suppress Syrians calling for democracy. While Moscow certainly has killed some known terrorists and helped reduce territory controlled by ISIS, it has also strengthened other terrorists. Its reckless methods and support for Assad the butcher destroyed any chance of Russia being an effective counterterrorism partner with us.

Russia's indiscriminate bombing has targeted hospitals, schools, convoys, and rescue crews, like the heroic White Helmets. Its campaign of terror drove once moderate Syrians to embrace extremist groups that also fight Assad and his backers.

Despite our success in retaking key ISIS strongholds, Russian officials claim the U.S. supports ISIS and consistently threatens our forces in Syria.

(1)

Meanwhile, new Russian-made military equipment is increasingly showing up in the hands of Iranian-backed terrorist groups like the notorious Hezbollah.

Even more dangerous, Russia is effectively carving an Iranian-controlled corridor that stretches from Tehran to the borders of Israel, threatening our valued ally Israel.

Putin is laying the foundation for chronic instability in this vital part of the world. Moscow cannot be our partner so long as it continues to enable the terrorist state Iran, prop up Assad, arm Israel's foes, and contribute to the slaughter and misery of millions of Syrians.

Syria is not the only place where the Kremlin is backing terrorism. Senior U.S. military officials have claimed that Russia is now arming its former enemies, the Afghan Taliban, providing them with machine guns and other medium-weight weapons.

We also know that Putin has backed violent separatists in Ukraine and Georgia in his bloody quest to bully and conquer his neighbors. He arms thugs, inflaming ethnic tensions, and secretly sends his own soldiers, the little green men, across the border. Putin is destabilizing countries that aspire to have closer ties with the West.

We should not be fooled. These separatists are not noble freedom fighters. Pro-Russian rebels in Ukraine have been accused by the U.N. of murder, kidnapping, and torture.

In the last 16 months, these separatists have used car bombs to target Ukrainian security guards, journalists, and Kremlin critics, and they continue to ignore cease-fire agreements. They are terrorists of a different stripe, but like jihadists, they believe they can achieve their political goals through violence and political terrorism.

This should be no surprise since their patron, the Kremlin, uses terror to maintain its own grip on power. Putin routinely orders the assassination of political opponents and journalists exposing his corruption. According to U.S. intelligence officials, at least 14 mysterious deaths are suspected to be linked to the Kremlin that occurred in the U.K. alone.

Russian terrorism has even struck this city, the Nation's capital, Washington, DC. In 2015, Putin's former media czar came here to meet with our Justice Department and to discuss issues that were common to the United States and to what this individual had to say and share the inner workings of the Kremlin's propaganda machine.

Mysteriously, he never made it to the meeting. Instead, he was found dead from blunt force injuries. Investigators ruled it an accident, but members of the FBI have claimed otherwise.

This is unacceptable. The pattern of prominent Russians and Kremlin critics who end up dead under shady circumstances is impossible to ignore. The fact that Putin's terror has reached our shores should be taken seriously by Americans.

Russia does have a serious Islamic problem, there should be no mistake about it. Since 1970, more than 3,500 Russians are believed to have been killed in over 800 terrorist attacks. Islamic radicals from Chechnya have conducted attacks across Russia, including the 2004 Beslan school massacre that murdered 300 people.

ISIS has also struck at Russia, blowing up a Russian charter plane over the Sinai in 2015.

According to a recent report, Russia is the largest source, however, of foreign fighters in Syria and Iraq.

With this shared threat, the United States and Putin should be able to be natural allies against terrorism—but Putin's brutal conduct and persistent ambition to rival the U.S. has made Russia a state sponsor of terrorism. Putin arms terrorists like the Taliban, Hezbollah, and thugs around the world so long as they advance his personal goals to undermine democracy and challenge America.

It is time we see Putin for what he is. He is an international terrorist.

And I will yield to the ranking member on the subcommittee, from Massachusetts, Mr. Keating, for his opening statement.

Mr. KEATING. Thank you, Mr. Chairman, for calling this hearing today on Russia and the question of whether Russia can be a reliable counterterrorism partner to the United States.

It is important because what we are talking about are human lives at stake. These are our servicemen and -women overseas risking their lives to fight terrorism. These are our neighbors and loved ones. We just had an attack in New York City 1 week ago where eight innocent lives were taken.

They are our children studying abroad, our friends, family members finally taking that trip to Europe where our allies have suffered far too many horrific terrorist attacks. They are the brave law enforcement and first responders who run toward the attack when everyone else is running away from it.

Today we are here to talk about who we trust to protect the people we care about most. If we choose to partner with another country to fight terrorism we need to know we are fighting with the same people in mind and the same goals. I think we have all seen and were touched by the illustration after the attacks in Brussels last year that showed a tearful French flag comforting a tearful Belgian flag.

A strong terrorism partner knows what is at stake and fights alongside you so that both countries can be safer. We have strong allies fighting terrorism. We have partners who we can trust with our intelligence and who, when we put our own men and women in harm's way to make us safer, do not actively undermine their safety and counteract their hard-fought efforts to reduce the threat of terrorism.

So the question at hand today is, can Russia be one of those partners? Sure, there are instances where Russian self-interest happens to intersect with ours, and absolutely we should continue working toward better deconfliction when our militaries are both operating in the same space.

But that is not what makes a true ally. When you head into a foxhole together, it is pretty important you make sure you know the guy or gal who is in there with you.

Well, Russia, Russia attacked the United States. Russia set out in a coordinated plan to undermine and influence our democracy, the very heart of what it means to be an American. The Russian Government, the very government this administration is arguing should be our partner on counterterrorism, did this through spreading lies, through actual attacks on our voting systems in 21 states. And as egregious as that is, it is not over yet.

Allies do not attack each other. What we are uncovering as we learn more about the Russian efforts to infiltrate American social media is that their efforts are robust and they are calculated. This is not some random account here or there. This is a profound effort by a foreign country to attack the very underpinnings of our democracy and our right to live freely in it.

These are attacks on our country, let's call it what it is, because when we look our servicemen and -women in the eyes, we should be completely honest about who we are trusting as partners to keep them and us safe.

Pretty soon we will have been at war in the fight against terrorism for two decades. Within its first year in office this administration has signed the orders to send more troops to Afghanistan.

Well, we have a crystal clear illustration of what it means to have Russia as a counterterrorism partner by looking at Afghanistan. As we send more of our own, our children, our spouses, our friends, off to fight for greater security and stability, Russia is quite literally counteracting our efforts through their support of the Taliban, and through the Taliban, al-Qaeda.

This is not some tricky geopolitical, international relations game theory puzzle. This is a question of who is going to have our back when our women and men are in the field; who is going to work to minimize the resources we expend in this fight because we are fighting for the same goal of eliminating terrorism together.

But Russia has time and time again been willing to risk the safety of our men and women in uniform, and through their apparently never-ending attacks on our democracy would rather undermine our stability and security and weaken us than work together with us to make a stronger counterterrorism partner.

So we must ask, why are we convening this congressional hearing today? Well, we are asking this question because the President of the United States keeps giving the wrong answer, and we should be very concerned about his answer.

We should be concerned that new discoveries in the Trump-Russian investigations, like the Russian attacks on our democracy, keep coming to light. I believe the most recent numbers I have seen now: There are nine individuals with proximity to the now President who had contacts with Russia during the campaign and transition. There are indictments now in the special counsel's investigation into the campaign. And we seem to never stop learning about more concerning ties between Russia and this administration, including those still serving.

We owe it to every victim of terrorism and to every individual we are working to ensure never becomes a victim of terrorism, we owe it to our servicemen and -women and every American that we represent here in Congress to be very careful when we choose who we are going to trust as a partner in fighting terrorism.

Russia has failed time and time again to demonstrate it shares our goal of a safe and secure America. Frankly, it just doesn't add up how this administration can still be suggesting that Russia can be our partner in this fight when Russia is so intent on fighting us.

I would like to thank the witnesses for joining us on this important topic.

And, Mr. Chairman, I yield back.

Mr. POE. I thank the gentleman from Massachusetts.

I will yield to Mr. Rohrabacher from California, who is the chairman of the Europe, Eurasia, and Emerging Threats Subcommittee, for his opening remarks.

Mr. ROHRABACHER. Yes, thank you, Chairman Poe, and thank you for initiating this hearing today. I am happy to be part of what I think will be an important discussion, even though I obviously disagree with everything that has just been said.

In my subcommittee, I held a hearing on a similar topic just over 2 years ago. Since then, we have a new President in the White House who is, as we have just heard, genuinely interested to see if relations with Russia can be improved, as compared to the last 10 years of unrelenting hostility from the United States toward Russia.

I believe that the fact that our President wants to seek out and try to see if there are areas we can actually cooperate in—I think that is a good thing. I think it is a positive development for both of our countries.

It is significant that today is the 100th anniversary of the Bolshevik Revolution, a date which reminds us of the dark and bloody Soviet history. And I am proud that I played a significant part in the destruction of the Bolshevik regime that controlled the Soviet Union up until Ronald Reagan ended the Cold War as it should have been ended, peacefully, and reaching out to those people—and standing up, I might add, as well.

In Afghanistan, which has been mentioned, I seem to remember who armed the Taliban. I seem to remember who armed and organized the Taliban, Pakistan and Saudi Arabia. Yet I have never heard so much volatileness that maybe the Russians—I don't know what the Russians are doing in Afghanistan. I am going to be very interested in hearing our witnesses on that.

So, although there are those who would treat Russia today as if it were still the Soviet Union, that period of time is now behind us, thank God. Although the flaws of the current Russian Government are evident, as we have heard some described in these last few moments, it behooves us to recognize that there has been a major change in what Russia was when it was the Soviet Union, a head of a Communist government that was seeking to create atheist dictatorships throughout the world. When Russia was the Soviet Union it was thus our primary enemy. One thing Ronald Reagan did is he prioritized: That is our primary enemy. What is the goal? Our goal is we win and they lose—they come down.

Now that enemy today is no longer the Soviet Union and now it is Russia who is there, but it is not our primary enemy. Radical Islamic terrorism—we just heard that 3,500 Russians were killed by terrorist activity in the last decade, okay, that is a lot of people—so Islamic terrorism threatens both the United States and Russia. And we might add that we have heard the figure, the largest group of members in Syria of the ISIL and those groups that are fighting there come from Chechnya, Russia.

No wonder there is something that tells the Russians they need to pay attention to this. But we should be working with them to try to create a more peaceful situation and defeat the radical Islamic terrorists that threaten both of us and are the basic problem in the Middle East.

So I think there are great opportunities for cooperation, and they should not be passed up because of basically what I have seen as hostility, hostility, hostility toward any idea of cooperating with the Russians for the last 10 years.

The fight against violent radical Islam is the major threat of our time. As we saw last week in the streets of Manhattan, the threat of radical Islam is pervasive. Radicalized Muslims have slaughtered innocents not just in the Middle East, but in Europe. And yes, as we have just heard, 3,500 in Russia—not counting the airplanes that were shot down over the Sinai Desert filled with Russian tourists.

These terrorists have declared war on modern and Western civilization. The future of America and Russia and, yes, Western civilization depends on the defeat of this enemy.

We have been in this spot before. We took on that threat to Western civilization. It was called Nazism, the Nazis. How did we defeat the Nazis? Yeah, we actually reached out to Joseph Stalin. Yeah, we defeated Nazism, and then we defeated Communism. And we will defeat radical Islam, but we have got to prioritize our effort and quit this, as I say, unrelenting hostility toward Russia and anybody who is their ally.

In the aftermath of the Boston bombing in May 2013—and I will say that you went with me to that hearing, that meeting that we had in Moscow—we met with the Russian Government and with Russian intelligence officials to discuss the threat of terrorism. They actually gave us the documents that they sent. And they also gave us other documents that had they sent—had it been a more of a—I can't do an opening statement? Okay. Anyway——

Mr. POE. You can do an opening statement.

Mr. ROHRABACHER. But not longer. Okay. I will finish up.

Let me just say, we were given an example of cooperation. Had we been cooperating at a heavy level at that time that we could have been doing we would have probably been able to stop that slaughter at the Boston Marathon. They had further information that would have alerted us to that.

That is the type of thing we can do. That is the type of thing that we should be reaching out and trying to cooperate with, rather than simply trying to state what we believe is an analysis of the Russian wrongdoing, which some of this is very debatable.

So with that said, thank you, Mr. Poe. Sorry I took so long.

Mr. POE. Thank you, Mr. Rohrabacher.

The Chair yields to the ranking member, Mr. Meeks from New York. You have 5 minutes for your opening statement.

Mr. MEEKS. Thank you, Chairman Poe, for holding this hearing to provide us with an opportunity to discuss counterterror cooperation between the U.S. and Russia. And I am almost tempted to go off of what I wanted to say in listening to my good friend, the chairman of our subcommittee.

Mr. ROHRABACHER. We are buddies. Don't worry about it.

Mr. MEEKS. I am going to try to stay disciplined because I think that the facts as we look at them today and as we found from every—just about all of our intelligence sources that there are some other things that is going on in Russia.

When you think about it, it is great that we are having a hearing now, particularly with the expert panel that we have, including people who have worked on U.S. policy to cooperate with Russia in an area of similarly mutual benefit, you would think, on common sense, maybe it makes sense. The timing is also perfect for us to debate the merits of potential cooperation in Syria, as well.

So on the surface, yes, you can say you can see Russia as a potential partner in many areas—cultural issues, trade, for example—not only on counterterror efforts. And I am a firm believer, as many know, in multilateral efforts to solve the world's problems.

However, it would be naive to promote a policy of cooperation in counterterror efforts without a sober understanding of today's Russia and the history of attempts to cooperate and establish clear goals that incorporate and leverage our allies across the globe.

Russia faces a problem of internal extremism related to its history first of brutality suppressing the Chechnyans, Russian citizens, in the 1990s. Journalists who bravely investigated this were killed and the situation remains a cauldron for Moscow.

This is where today's Russian leadership honed its counterterror strategy that it uses abroad today. The strategy can be seen on display in its scorched earth policies in Syria and the funneling of fighters from Chechnya to other areas of conflict in the region, including the Ukraine.

Given the Kremlin's cooperation with the Iranians in Syria and its support for a larger Shia crescent, where can we find common interests? I don't know. If anything, in Syria we should call it deconfliction and not cooperation.

Indeed, while the Obama administration moved forward with its reset policy, counterterror cooperation was on the table. Instead, there was a demonstrable lack of interest in deep cooperation from the Russian side. And I believe that some who will testify today, we will hear that from them, they will talk about that.

We learned from the experience, however, about the motives of this cooperation. Any proposed cooperation would give the Kremlin cover for its indiscriminate bombing in Syria, and thereby stroke anti-American feelings in the region. It would put us then on the side of the Shias in Iran. Finally, it would give Russia generous inroads for its intelligence services—not as counterterror experts.

So does this mean we stop talking to Moscow or looking for areas to cooperate? No, I don't think so. But let us recognize the unfortunate limitations of today's Kremlin. Let us put Putin's dreams of grand bargains to the side. Let us strive to promote peace by supporting our allies in the Middle East and Europe; let us not fall for the games.

I agree. At one time I thought that, as Mr. Rohrabacher talked about, you are no longer the Soviet Union, we can do certain things. Well, clearly, that was not the opinion of Mr. Putin. And he has shown over and over by what has happened in the United States and what has been happening in Europe, and you talk to our European allies, that the areas of cooperation are very limited because what he wants to do is make you think one thing while they do something else.

So, I look forward to honestly assessing the potential areas for cooperation with the Kremlin, and I look forward to a robust conversation with our esteemed panel to get a back and forth on this very important issue. And I yield back.

Mr. POE. I thank the gentleman from New York.

Without objection, all witnesses' statements will be made part of the record. I ask that each witness limit their presentation to no more than 5 minutes. All members of both subcommittees have copies of your written testimony and had so before this hearing this afternoon.

I will introduce each witness and give them time for their statements.

Dr. Colin Clarke is a political scientist at the RAND Corporation where he focuses on terrorism, insurgency, and criminal networks. In addition, he is an associate fellow at the International Center for Counterterrorism and lecturer at the Carnegie Mellon University.

Dr. Svante Cornell is the director of the Central Asia-Caucasus Institute at the American Foreign Policy Council. He is also the co-founder of the Institute for Security and Development Policy in Stockholm.

Mr. Simon Saradzhyan is the founding director of the Russia Matters Project at Harvard Kennedy School's Belfer Center for Science and International Affairs. He previously worked as a consultant and journalist in Russia for 15 years.

Dr. Michael Carpenter is the senior director of the Penn Biden Center for Diplomacy and Global Engagement and a nonresident fellow at the Atlantic Council. Dr. Carpenter previously served in the Pentagon as a Deputy Assistant Secretary of Defense with responsibility for Russia, Ukraine, Eurasia, Balkans, and conventional arms control.

Dr. Clarke, we will start with you. You have 5 minutes.

STATEMENT OF COLIN P. CLARKE, PH.D., POLITICAL SCIENTIST, RAND CORPORATION

Mr. CLARKE. Thank you, Chairman Poe and Ranking Member Keating, Chairman Rohrabacher and Ranking Member Meeks, and distinguished members of the subcommittee for inviting me to testify today.

Throughout my testimony I will highlight the following areas. First, Russia's recent history with jihadist terrorism. Second, Russian counterinsurgency and counterterrorism tactics and strategy in the Caucasus. Third, the potential backlash from Russia's foray into Syria and its military campaign there. Fourth, what the future might hold for Russia now that ISIS' caliphate has collapsed. I will conclude with implications that Russia's struggle with jihadist terrorism has for the United States.

On recent history, Russia's modern trouble with Islamic militancy dates back to the Soviet invasion of Afghanistan in 1979. Throughout the former Soviet Union, as well as in areas like Chechnya and others along Russia's southern flank, civil war and conflicts raged, many of which were fueled by militant groups inspired by religion and active throughout the Caucasus in Central Asia.

Even beyond the battlefields of the Caucasus, Islamic militants have launched many high profile attacks on Russian soil, including one specifically targeting transportation infrastructure.

Militants have also conducted spectacular attacks, meticulously planned operations specifically designed to kill civilians and spread terror throughout the population, such as the Moscow theater hostage crisis in 2002 and the Beslan school siege in 2004.

On Russian COIN and counterterrorism. During the first Chechnyan war—from 1994 to 1996—the Russian military followed a scorched earth policy of destroying everything in sight. Chechnya's capital, Grozny, was completely besieged by Russian artillery and indiscriminate bombing. Russian counterinsurgency strategy in the Caucasus has frequently employed zachistkas, or mop-up operations, designed to kill or capture terrorists and their supporters although noncombatants are often caught up in these sweeps. Other tactics have included forced disappearances, collective punishment, and the targeting of suspected insurgents' families, friends, and neighbors.

This heavy-handed approach is myopic. It trades longer-term stability for short-term security as the domestic population in large swaths of the Caucasus has been traumatized by extrajudicial killings, torture, and widespread assassinations.

In line with Russia's seeming refusal to even attempt to win hearts and minds, the insurgents' social, political, and economic grievances have largely been ignored; practically ensuring that future generations of militants will pick up the mantle of jihad.

Russia's focus has been largely kinetic, as the military has relied on its capitation strategy to eliminate successive high-ranking insurgent military commanders over the years.

On backlash from Syria—Russia has been one of the primary forces propping up the Assad regime, which has ruthlessly targeted its opponents, most of whom are Sunnis, with barrel bombs and chemical weapons.

Russia and Iran are also deepening their political and military alliance as their respective militaries work together to help Assad reclaim pockets of territory from opposition forces. Russian special forces and warplanes serve as a force multiplier for Hezbollah fighters who have bloodied Sunni militants in battle. Moscow's desire to expand Russian influence in the Middle East has pitted it squarely against Sunnis and their interests.

For Russia, the demographics are also daunting. There are thousands of Russian citizens fighting with ISIS and another 5,000 to 7,000 Russian-speaking jihadists, making Russia the second-most popular language spoken within ISIS. This means that Sunni jihadist groups have a ready-made native force capable of returning back home to Russia where militants can more easily blend in with local populations.

With respect to what the future holds, Russia's deepening involvement in Syria means that Moscow has essentially chosen sides in a sectarian conflict abroad, a strategy that could lead to tragedy at home. A new report by the Soufan Group estimates that Russia is indeed the largest exporter of foreign fighters to the conflicts in Iraq and Syria, with more than 3,200 fighters.

One factor that could play a significant role in the scale and scope of the threat facing Russia in the future is the struggle for supremacy between jihadist groups in the Caucasus. A competition for recruits and resources is intensifying between the two dominant jihadist entities, fostering decentralization of the insurgency.

In its quest to become more assertive geopolitically by assuming a more aggressive role abroad, Russia has made itself more vulnerable to terrorism at home. Still, Putin could see the threat of Sunni militancy at home as the inevitable tradeoff for restoring Russian hegemony in its former sphere of influence and bringing the country back to what he views as its rightful place as a true global power.

Any Russian attempts to compare the Russian campaign against jihadists with America's war on terrorism would be inaccurate. Russia has never been an equal partner in the fight against Islamic extremism. Moreover, Russia has too often exacerbated the global problem through brutal reprisals and an iron fist response to Islamic communities within its own borders.

Accordingly, the United States should not view Russia as a viable counterterrorism partner at present. Any efforts to cooperate in this area should be judicious, measured, and treated with the requisite degree of skepticism it deserves.

Thank you for the opportunity to testify today.

[The prepared statement of Mr. Clarke follows:]

Testimony

Jihadist Violence in the Caucasus

Russia Between Counterterrorism and Counterinsurgency

Colin P. Clarke

CT-483

Testimony presented before the House Foreign Affairs Committee, Subcommittee on Terrorism, Nonproliferation, and Trade and Subcommittee on Europe, Eurasia, and Emerging Threats on November 7, 2017.

12

For more information on this publication, visit www.rand.org/pubs/testimonies/CT483.html

Testimonies

RAND testimonies record testimony presented or submitted by RAND associates to federal, state, or local legislative committees; government-appointed commissions and panels; and private review and oversight bodies.

www.rand.org

Jihadist Violence in the Caucasus: Russia Between Counterterrorism and Counterinsurgency

Testimony of Colin Clarke[1]
The RAND Corporation[2]

Before the Committee on Foreign Affairs
Subcommittee on Terrorism, Nonproliferation, and Trade
Subcommittee on Europe, Eurasia, and Emerging Threats
United States House of Representatives

November 7, 2017

Like the United States, Russia has suffered at the hands of Islamic militants. But although our enemies might be motivated by a similar ideology, in the long term, the United States and Russia have starkly different objectives. The United States seeks the defeat of the Islamic State of Iraq and Syria (ISIS), an end to the war in Syria, and the stabilization of countries on the periphery of the North Atlantic Treaty Organization (NATO). Russia, meanwhile, seeks to project power into the Middle East, rebuild its former sphere of influence along NATO's borders, foment instability in pro-Western nations, and keep the United States bogged down in ongoing conflicts to attenuate U.S. resources and morale. Russia's invasion of Georgia, annexation of Crimea, and intervention in Syria, as well as recent efforts to aid the Taliban, are proof of these objectives.[3]

In the immediate aftermath of the September 11, 2001, terrorist attacks, Russia trumpeted its counterterrorism cooperation with America to root out al Qaeda. After all, Russia has dealt with

---

[1] The opinions and conclusions expressed in this testimony are the author's alone and should not be interpreted as representing those of the RAND Corporation or any of the sponsors of its research.

[2] The RAND Corporation is a research organization that develops solutions to public policy challenges to help make communities throughout the world safer and more secure, healthier and more prosperous. RAND is nonprofit, nonpartisan, and committed to the public interest.

[3] Nick Paton Walsh and Mamoud Popalzai, "Videos Suggest Russian Government May be Arming Taliban," *CNN*, July 26, 2017.

its own share of attacks launched by Islamic militants and has waged a counterinsurgency throughout the Caucasus against a protean network of militants. Over the years, attacks against Russia proper have largely been launched by local Sunni groups with varying levels of religious fervor, from those more focused on ethno-nationalist concerns to those determined to spread sharia law throughout the Caucasus. The jihadist campaign of protracted violence has permeated the region and has included not only attacks in the heart of Russia, but also more traditional insurgent actions throughout Dagestan, Ingushetia, and other areas throughout southern Russia.

Well before Russia drew the ire of Salafi jihadists for intervening in Syria, long-simmering insurgencies on Russian soil have been met with iron-fisted counterinsurgency operations. The Russians have waged a ruthless military campaign against a patchwork of Sunni militants from Ingushetia to Ossetia in the Caucasus.[4] And while Russia's counterinsurgency and counterterrorism strategy has been relatively effective in the short term, the draconian tactics employed by Russian forces could prove counterproductive in the long run, alienating substantial portions of the population and adding to significant grievances exploitable by Salafi jihadists.

Throughout my testimony, I will highlight the following areas:

- first, Russia's recent history with jihadist terrorism, dating back to the end of the Cold War and its incursions into Chechnya
- second, Russian counterinsurgency and counterterrorism tactics and strategy in the Caucasus
- third, the potential backlash from Russia's foray into Syria and its military campaign there
- fourth, what the future might hold for Russia now that ISIS's caliphate has collapsed and potentially thousands of Russian and Russian-speaking foreign fighters could be leaving the battlefield in the Middle East, perhaps heading for new destinations, including Russia or countries on its borders.

I will conclude with the implications of Russia's struggle with jihadist terrorism has for the United States, namely in terms of potential areas of cooperation.

Recent Russian History with Jihadist Terrorism

Russia's modern trouble with Islamic militancy dates back to the Soviet invasion of Afghanistan in 1979. Throughout the former Soviet Union, including in areas like Chechnya as well as along Russia's southern flank, civil war and conflicts raged, many of which were fueled by militant groups inspired by religion and active throughout the Caucasus and Central Asia. Russia fought two bloody wars in Chechnya. The first lasted from 1994 to 1996, while the Second Chechen War flared back up in 1999 and lasted on and off for a decade. Throughout the 1990s, myriad anti-Russian rebel groups adopted more religious ideologies. Many scholars attribute this shift to the growing influence of foreign fighters from the Middle East and Central Asia, including the Ibn al-Khattab battalion.[5]

---

[4] Stephen J. Blank, *Russia's Homegrown Insurgency: Jihad in the North Caucasus*, Carlisle Barracks, Penn.: U.S. Army War College Strategic Studies Institute, October 24, 2012.

[5] Leah Farrall, "How Al Qaeda Works," *Foreign Affairs*, March/April 2011.

Even beyond the battlefields of the Caucasus, Islamic militants have launched many high-profile attacks on Russian soil, including ones specifically targeting transportation infrastructure—suicide bombings in the Moscow Metro in 2004 and 2010, an explosion that derailed the Moscow–St. Petersburg express railroad in 2007, and suicide attacks on the Domodedovo Airport in 2011 and on a bus in Volgograd in 2013.[6] Militants have also conducted spectacular attacks—meticulously planned operations specifically designed to kill civilians and spread terror throughout the population—such as the Moscow theater hostage crisis in 2002 and the Beslan school siege in 2004.

More recently, in April of this year, explosions tore through a tunnel between the Sennaya Ploshchad and Tekhnologichesky Institut stations in the St. Petersburg metro system, killing at least ten.[7] The bomber was later identified as Akbarzhon Jalilov, an ethnic Uzbek from Kyrgyzstan.[8] Russia has also been attacked beyond its territory, as evidenced by the bombing of Metrojet flight 9268 by an ISIS affiliate after the plane departed Sharm El-Sheikh for St. Petersburg in October 2015.[9] All 224 people on the plane, mostly Russian citizens, died in the attack.

Russian Counterterrorism and Counterinsurgency

During the First Chechen War, from 1994 to 1996, the Russian military followed a scorched-earth policy of destroying everything in sight.[10] Chechnya's capital, Grozny, was completely besieged by Russian artillery and indiscriminate bombing. Russian counterinsurgency strategy in the Caucasus has frequently employed *zachistkas*, or mop-up operations, designed to kill or capture terrorists and their supporters, although noncombatants are often caught up in these sweeps.[11] Other tactics have included forced disappearances; collective punishment; and the targeting of suspected insurgents' families, friends, and neighbors. Despite widespread accusations of human rights abuses during the course of counterterrorism operations, Russian propaganda seeks to craft an image of the Russian state as a protector of the people. Russian President Vladimir Putin also regularly conflates anti-Russian insurgents with the global jihadist movement, even though some have no actual connections and for others, linkages can be tenuous at best.

---

[6] Luke Harding and Tom Parfitt. "Domodedovo Airport Hit By Deadly Bombing," *The Guardian,* January 24, 2011.

[7] Colin P. Clarke, "How Russia Became the Jihadists' No. 1 Target," *Politico,* April 3, 2017.

[8] Saim Saeed, "At Least 10 Killed in St. Petersburg Metro Blasts," *Politico,* April 3, 2017; Ivan Nechepurenko and Neil MacFarquhar, "Explosion in St. Petersburg, Russia, Kills 11 as Vladimir Putin Visits," *New York Times,* April 3, 2017; and "St. Petersburg Metro Bombing a Possible Suicide Attack," *BBC News,* April 4, 2017.

[9] Joseph Krauss, "Islamic State Releases Photo of Bomb It Says Downed Russian Jet, Claims Killing of 2 Hostages," *U.S. News & World Report,* November 19, 2015.

[10] Mark Kramer, "The Perils of Counterinsurgency: Russia's War in Chechnya," *International Security,* Vol. 29, No. 3, Winter 2004/2005, pp. 5–63; see also Christopher Paul, Colin P. Clarke, and Beth Grill, *Victory Has a Thousand Fathers: Detailed Counterinsurgency Case Studies,* Santa Monica, Calif.: RAND Corporation, MG-964/1-OSD, 2010, pp. 253–263.

[11] Brian Glyn Williams, *Inferno in Chechnya: The Russian-Chechen Wars, the Al Qaeda Myth, and the Boston Marathon Bombings,* Lebanon, N.H.: Foredge, 2015, p. 183.

While Russia's authoritarian approach to counterinsurgency could be considered effective in quelling low-intensity conflict, its methods are brutal.[12] This heavy-handed approach is myopic—it trades longer-term stability for short-term security—as the domestic population in large swaths of the Caucasus has been traumatized by extrajudicial killings, torture, and widespread assassinations.[13] In line with Russia's seeming refusal to even attempt to "win hearts and minds," the insurgents' social, political, and economic grievances have largely been ignored, practically ensuring that future generations of militants will pick up the mantle of jihad. Russia's focus has been largely kinetic, as the military has relied on a decapitation strategy to eliminate successive high-ranking insurgent military commanders over the years.[14]

Russia has been battling various domestic militant groups for years, but the state of political violence in the Caucasus has changed in important ways over the past two decades. To rule Chechnya, Putin installed strongman Ramzan Kadyrov, whose co-option of former militants has decreased violence in the region.[15] In turn, the center of gravity of the insurgency has shifted from Chechnya to Dagestan, with ISIS's Caucasus Governorate holding sway in those two territories as well as others nearby—Kabarda, Balkaria and Karachay—while the al Qaeda-affiliated Caucasus Emirate clings to its turf in Cherkessia and Nogay Steppe.[16]

In the lead-up to the 2014 Winter Olympics in Sochi, Russian authorities encouraged Sunni militants to depart for Syria to wage jihad.[17] The thought process behind this encouragement was simple, if underhanded—militants would leave for Syria, and stout Russian border controls—or the Russian Air Force—would ensure they never returned.[18] Despite this encouragement, Putin has expressed concern about the possibility of jihadists returning from Syria, noting that these militants will not simply "vanish into thin air."[19] Moreover, Russia's approach to counterinsurgency eschews addressing grievances, instead relying almost exclusively on military force.[20] This means that the root causes of the political violence go largely ignored, allowing the ideology fueling militant Salafists to fester indefinitely.

---

[12] Daniel Byman, "Death Solves All Problems: The Authoritarian Counterinsurgency Tool Kit," *War on the Rocks,* February 3, 2016; see also Thomas E. Ricks. "Counterinsurgency: The Brutal But Effective Russian Approach," *Foreign Policy,* September 17, 2009.

[13] Colin P. Clarke, "Attacks on Russia Will Only Increase," *The Atlantic,* April 4, 2017.

[14] International Crisis Group, "The North Caucasus Insurgency and Syria: An Exported Jihad?" March 16, 2016. Some of these leaders include include Dzokhar Dudaev (1996), Zelimkhan Yaderbiyev (1997), Aslan Maskhadov (2005), Abdul-Halim Sadulayev (2006), and Doku Umarov (2013).

[15] Derek Henry Flood, "The Islamic State Raises Its Black Flag Over the Caucasus," *CTC Sentinel,* June 29, 2015.

[16] David M. Herszenhorn and Andrew Roth. "Search for Home Led Suspect to Land Marred by Strife," *New York Times,* April 21, 2013; see also Derek Henry Flood, "The Caucasus Emirate: From Anti-Colonial Roots to Salafi-Jihad," *CTC Sentinel,* March 26, 2014; and Harleen Gambhir, "ISIS Declares Governorate in Russia's North Caucasus Region," Institute for the Study of War, June 23, 2015.

[17] Maria Tsvetkova, "How Russia Allowed Homegrown Radicals to Go and Fight in Syria," *Reuters,* May 13, 2016.

[18] Michael Weiss, "Russia's Double Game with Islamic Terror," *Daily Beast,* August 23, 2015.

[19] Flood, 2014.

[20] International Crisis Group, 2016.

Potential Backlash Against Russian Actions

Recent Russian actions in the Middle East—including its escalating intervention in Syria and its moves toward intervention in Libya, with the recent deployment of special forces to an air base in Egypt—have drawn the ire of militant Sunnis worldwide.[21] Russia is increasingly perceived as a vanguard of Shia interests.[22] Putin has provided substantial military aid to Syrian leader Bashar al-Assad, allying Russia with Shia Iran and Lebanese Hezbollah, avowed enemies of Sunni jihadists.

In an ISIS video titled "Soon Very Soon Blood Will Spill Like an Ocean," an ISIS fighter threatens Putin directly, citing the country's intervention in Syria and its growing alliance with Assad, Iran, and the Lebanese Hezbollah as proof that Moscow is the chief proponent of a growing Shia axis throughout the Middle East.[23] Practically, following the recapture of Raqqa, thousands of Russian foreign fighters could attempt to return home, dramatically worsening the situation for Moscow.[24]

Russia has been one of the primary forces propping up the Assad regime, which has ruthlessly targeted its opponents (most of whom are Sunnis) with barrel bombs and chemical weapons. Russia and Iran are also deepening their political and military alliance, as their respective militaries work together to help Assad reclaim pockets of territory from opposition forces.[25] Russian Special Forces and warplanes serve as a force multiplier for Hezbollah fighters who have bloodied Sunni militants in battle.[26] Moscow's desire to expand Russian influence in the Middle East has pitted it squarely against Sunnis and their interests. For Russia, the demographics are also daunting. There are thousands of Russian citizens fighting with ISIS, and another 5,000 to 7,000 Russian-speaking jihadists, making Russian the second most-popular language spoken within ISIS.[27] This means that Sunni jihadist groups have a ready-made, native force capable of returning back home to Russia, where militants can more easily blend in with local populations while plotting further attacks.

---

[21] Phil Stewart, Idrees Ali, and Lin Noueihed, "Russia Appears to Deploy Forces to Egypt, Eyes on Libya Role," *Reuters,* March 13, 2017.

[22] Leon Aron, "The Coming of the Russian Jihad: Part II," *War on the Rocks,* December 19, 2016b.

[23] Salma Abdelaziz and Alex Felton, "ISIS Threatens Russia in New Video," *CNN,* November 12, 2015; see also Neil MacFarquhar, "For Russia, Links Between Caucasus and ISIS Provoke Anxiety," *New York Times,* November 20, 2015; Aron, 2016b; and Brian Glyn Williams and Robert Souza, "The Consequences of Russia's 'Counterterrorism' Campaign," *CTC Sentinel,* November 30, 2016.

[24] Leon Aron, "The Coming of the Russian Jihad: Part I," *War on the Rocks,* September 23, 2016a.

[25] Mohsen Milani, "Iran and Russia's Uncomfortable Alliance," *Foreign Affairs,* August 31, 2016.

[26] Jesse Rosenfeld, "Russia is Arming Hezbollah, Say Two of the Group's Field Commanders," *Daily Beast,* January 11, 2016.

[27] Aron, 2016a.

Conclusion: What Might the Future Hold?

Russia's deepening involvement in Syria means that Moscow has essentially chosen sides in a sectarian conflict abroad—a strategy that could lead to tragedy at home. A new report by the Soufan Group estimates that Russia is indeed the largest exporter of foreign fighters to the conflicts in Iraq and Syria, with more than 3,200 fighters.[28] Many citizens of the former Soviet states rose through the ranks to become leaders within militant groups fighting in Syria, including the now-deceased Tarkhan Batirashvili, more commonly known as Abu Omar al-Shishani—"Omar the Chechen," the former ISIS minister of war.[29]

One factor that could play a significant role in the scale and scope of the threat facing Russia in the future is the struggle for supremacy between jihadist groups in the Caucasus. A competition for recruits and resources is intensifying between the two dominant jihadist entities, fostering decentralization of the insurgency.[30]

In recent years, many high-ranking jihadists have switched allegiance from the Caucasus Emirate to Wilayat Qawqaz.[31] ISIS, in their eyes, is the most legitimate force espousing the austere brand of Salafism popular among jihadists, particularly the younger generation. The split between the two groups will continue to manifest, likely resulting in a process of outbidding, in which violent nonstate groups rely on spectacular attacks to persuade potential acolytes that their terrorist or insurgent organization has a stronger resolve to fight the adversary—in this case, the Russian state and security services.[32] The competition has even extended to the battlefield in Syria, which has only heightened the stakes.

Despite the fallout and subsequent competition for recruits and resources between the al Qaeda-linked Caucasus Emirate and the ISIS-linked Wilayat Qawqaz, one issue with the potential to unite these feuding Sunni factions is a shared hatred of Shia—and their main patron, Russia.[33]

For all of the success of Russia's counterinsurgency campaign in Chechnya, counterterrorism is something different. While a counterinsurgency strategy can entail deploying vast numbers of soldiers using brute force, counterterrorism is essentially a law-enforcement discipline, driven by intelligence. Russia has proven that it is willing and able to employ brutal methods to defeat an insurgency, but has yet to demonstrate the capabilities necessary to deter and disrupt terrorist attacks on its soil, including devastating attacks on its transportation infrastructure.

---

[28] Richard Barrett, "Beyond the Caliphate: Foreign Fighters and the Threat of Returnees," *Soufan Group*, October 24, 2017; see also Jack Moore, "Russia Overtakes Saudi Arabia and Tunisia as Largest Exporter of ISIS Fighters," *Newsweek*, October 24, 2017.

[29] Eric Schmitt and Michael S. Schmidt, "Omar the Chechen, a Senior Leader in ISIS, Dies After U.S. Airstrike," *New York Times*, March 15, 2016.

[30] Andrew S. Bowen, "ISIS Comes to Russia," *Daily Beast*, July 10, 2015.

[31] Bowen, 2015.

[32] Andrew H. Kydd and Barbara F. Walter, "The Strategies of Terrorism," *International Security*, Vol.31, No.1, Summer 2006, pp.49-80.

[33] William McCants, "The Polarizing Effect of Islamic State Aggression on the Global Jihadist Movement," *CTC Sentinel*, July 27, 2016; see also Ekaterina Sokirianskaia, "Russia's North Caucasus Insurgency Widens as ISIS' Foothold Grows," *World Politics Review*, April 12, 2016.

In its quest to become more assertive geopolitically by assuming a more aggressive role abroad, Russia has made itself more vulnerable to terrorism at home. Sunni militants may see Russian actions in the Middle East and Eastern Europe and conclude that now, while Moscow is seemingly distracted, is the time to strike. ISIS and other jihadists could be preparing to take the fight to Russia's major cities in an attempt to prove their own relevance, while seeking to make good on repeated promises to make Putin and company pay for their misadventures in Muslim lands. Still, Putin could see the threat of Sunni militancy at home as the inevitable trade-off for restoring Russian hegemony in its former sphere of influence and bringing the country back to what he views as its rightful place as a true global power.

Any Russian attempts to compare the Russian campaign against jihadists with America's war on terrorism would be inaccurate. Russia has never been an equal partner in the fight against Islamic extremism – its military and intelligence services have little to offer. Moreover, Russia has too often exacerbated the global problem through brutal reprisals and an iron-fist response to Islamic communities within its own borders. Accordingly, the United States should not view Russia as a viable counterterrorism partner at present. Any effort to cooperate in this area should be judicious, measured, and treated with the requisite degree of skepticism it deserves.

———

Mr. POE. Thank you, Dr. Clarke.
Dr. Cornell.

STATEMENT OF SVANTE CORNELL, PH.D., SENIOR FELLOW FOR EURASIA, DIRECTOR OF THE CENTRAL ASIA-CAUCASUS INSTITUTE, AMERICAN FOREIGN POLICY COUNCIL

Mr. CORNELL. Thank you very much, Chairman Poe, Ranking Member Keating, Chairman Rohrabacher, Ranking Member Meeks, for the opportunity to testify today.

I would like to start by pointing out that I think there has been a bipartisan U.S. policy over the past decade or more to seek Russian cooperation on major international issues.

Obviously, this was the case with the Bush administration after 9/11 on Afghanistan, Iran, and on resolving unresolved conflicts in the Caucasus and the Caspian region.

The Obama administration's reset policy was obviously predicated on the assumption that Russia could be a partner on all of these issues and on Syria later on.

And the Trump administration has been to some extent influenced by thinking that Russia shares interests with the United States in fighting radical Islamic terrorism.

As several of the opening statements made clear, and I agree with that, Russian behavior suggests otherwise. I would argue that it suggests that Russia's main aim is to undermine U.S. leadership in the world, and when insurgents and terrorists contribute to this goal in one way or another, Russia has no problem with coordinating with them, support them, and of course, manipulate them.

Chairman Poe mentioned the conflict in Ukraine, and I think going further it is clear that a central instrument in Russian policy in the whole post-Soviet space has been the manipulation and sometimes creation of so-called frozen conflicts. We have seen this in Azerbaijan, Georgia, Moldova, and lately Ukraine. The first three cases, this was dating back to the early 1990s.

In Ukraine these conflicts were basically manufactured out of thin air. There were no preexisting conflicts that Russia interfered in—they created them to undermine the statehood of Ukraine.

Now, what do all the countries that are suffering from this problem have in common? They all are trying to escape from the Russian sphere of influence and looking to the United States for leadership in the world. The countries that have accepted the Russian sphere of influence, such as Belarus, such as Armenia, don't have a problem on their own territory with unresolved conflicts.

More vexing than this issue in Russia's neighborhood is Russia's attitude to Islamic terrorism. I would point out that Russia's support for insurgency extends directly to anti-American actors, including Islamic extremism.

Chairman Poe mentioned that in Afghanistan since 2015, we have reports of Russian support for the Taliban. Back then, a Russian official said that Russian interests objectively coincide with those of the Taliban. This Russian official claimed that the major purpose of that was opposing ISIS.

However, a senior Taliban official who was interviewed at the time said that Russia and the Taliban had been in contact since 2007, long before ISIS even existed, and that the main cause for that was the existence of the main enemy, the United States—and that Russia—also like the Taliban, wanted the United States out of Afghanistan.

Now, this obviously flies in the face of the notion that Russia has been a supporter in the U.S. efforts, war efforts in Afghanistan, because just while President Obama was lauding Russia for supporting a transportation network through Russia and Central Asia known as the Northern Distribution Network, Russia was already ramping up its support for the Taliban. As we know now, and as multiple U.S. high military officials have testified, this now includes arms deliveries and other types of support.

Ranking Member Meeks and the previous speaker mentioned Chechnya, and indeed the insurgency against Russian rule there in the 1990s was mainly a nationalist and a secular insurgency. The Chechnyan nationalists were viewed as quite a legitimate actor by many in the West, including on Capitol Hill, but gradually—after the 1994 to 1996 war—there was a radical Islamic component that emerged within Chechnya and within the North Caucasus.

Now, you would think that Russia would target this component rather than the nationalists and secularists with whom you would actually be able to negotiate, but in fact the opposite was true. As I detail in my written testimony, Russia actively worked to destroy particularly the nationalist and secular forces in the insurgency, and, in fact, bolstered directly and mainly indirectly, the Islamic extremist groups, some of which Russia had infiltrated and succeeded in manipulating. These are, by the way, some of the forces that are now in Syria.

And the purpose—and this becomes very relevant in the Syrian context—was basically to force everybody, ordinary Chechnyans, outsiders, including the United States, to confront a binary choice. Either you support Russia's own loyal Chechnyan administration or you are left with the radical Islamic terrorists and there is nothing in between.

Now, going to Syria, I mentioned Chechnya in particular because this is exactly the blueprint that Russia has presented to the world by its support for the Assad regime. By focusing its energies on destroying the moderate U.S.-supported parts of the insurgency that targeted Assad they leave ordinary Syrians and the rest of the world with, again, the same binary choice, either oppose Assad or you are left with ISIS.

Now, as I close, I would just like to reflect on why Russia is following this policy.

Now, Russia is ruled by a regime that is dominated not by the national interests, but by the regime interests of Mr. Putin and his allies, and the key regime interest is to create an international environment that is conducive to maintaining that system of government in Russia.

For this purpose, Western democracies, especially the United States, are a threat—not a military threat—but a threat to the survival of the Russian regime because of the attraction of the democratic system of government. And, therefore, there is an underlying aim of all of Russian policy to undermine U.S. leadership in the world and to undermine the legitimacy of the U.S. democracy.

That is why Russian media depicts the West as morally decadent and chaotic. That is why Russia interferes in U.S. elections. And that is not about supporting one candidate or another, it is about generating chaos and crippling the political system of this country.

And by definition, by the way, this means that if Russia supports one candidate prior to an election, the moment that that candidate wins, that is a candidate that Russia will now be undermining. And that is, by the way, why Russian trolls that had worked against Hillary Clinton's campaign shifted tack as soon as President Trump won the election and immediately began questioning the legitimacy of President Trump's election.

So to end, I would say that Russia actually holds a fairly weak hand in international affairs. They have a very vulnerable economy and a very vulnerable political system. They are playing, if you will, a very bad hand very well.

We, on the other hand, have a much stronger hand in international affairs, but we are not playing it as well as the Russians do—and I think it is time for the U.S.—if you will, to call the bluff that is Russia's foreign policy. Thank you.

[The prepared statement of Mr. Cornell follows:]

"Russia: Counterterrorism Partner or Fanning the Flames?"
Russia's Relationship to Insurgent and Terrorist Groups

Testimony to the Terrorism, Nonproliferation, and Trade Subcommittee

Committee on Foreign Affairs

U.S. House of Representatives

By Svante E. Cornell
Director, Central Asia-Caucasus Institute
American Foreign Policy Council
509 C St NE, Washington DC 20002

Insurgency, Terrorism, and Russia's Perspective on International Affairs

To understand Russia's approach to insurgent and terrorist groups, it is necessary to take a step back and consider Russia's perspective on international affairs more broadly, and how that contrasts with the U.S. and European approach to world politics.

American policies over the past decade and a half have rested on the recognition of Russia as a key global player, whose cooperation is crucial to managing key international issues. Beyond Russia's veto power in the UN Security Council, Russia has had a stake in many of the issues at the center of international relations in the past two decades. The U.S. considered Russia a key partner in the war on terrorism and in transit operations for the war in Afghanistan. Similarly, it was seen as a key partner to roll back the Iranian nuclear program. Western powers also sought Russia's cooperation to manage the unresolved conflicts in the post-Soviet space. Even after Russia's invasion of Georgia in 2008, the U.S., Russia and France continue to co-chair the negotiation process to resolve the Armenian-Azerbaijani conflict. And, of course, the Obama Administration thought Russia's influence over the Assad regime in Syria made its cooperation essential to western goals in that conflict.

Across these areas of interaction with Russia, western leaders have depicted relations with Russia in terms of a win-win situation, where the West and Russia share common interests. Where Russian behavior has suggested otherwise, Western diplomats have focused on explaining to Russia, and to the wider public, why Russia's "true" interests should lead it to cooperate with the West. In the many cases where these urges have proven futile, Western leaders have decided to "compartmentalize:" to seek to isolate areas of agreement from areas of disagreement. Until recently, western leaders have assumed that the Russian leaders, too, have honorable intentions, or at a minimum, operate with their own country's best interests in mind.

When even this approach has failed, as it invariably has, Western leaders have tended to seek explanations as much in their own behavior as in Russia's. If Moscow will not work with us, the reasoning goes, we must be doing something wrong. If Moscow does not trust us, we must seek ways to rebuild confidence – this was the assumption of the Obama Administration's "Reset" launched in 2009. Only as a last resort, and as a result of great frustration, have Western leaders concluded that their efforts have failed because Russian leaders' policies actively seek to undermine American interests and security.

Since Vladimir Putin came to power, Moscow's approach to international affairs has been based on a fundamentally different logic than the Western approach. The Russian leadership has focused on the task of rebuilding Russia's power and influence on the global scene – and in particular, in reasserting an exclusive sphere of influence over the former Soviet space " – but not only," to use former Russian president Dmitry Medvedev's phrase following the invasion of Georgia in 2008. Key to this ambition has been to reduce what Russian leaders view as the Western, and particularly American, "hegemony" in world affairs.

To a considerable extent, Russian leaders are informed by a worldview that sees the West, and particularly the United States, as an aggressive and arrogant force that seeks world domination at the expense of the marginalization of others. While U.S. actions in the Middle East may have contributed to this perception, it is by no means reserved for the United States: when the EU launched the Eastern Partnership, Russia saw this as a threat to its historical sphere of influence, and Foreign Minister Sergey Lavrov blamed the EU of trying to build a "sphere of influence."[1]

The character of the Russian government is an important factor in determining its international behavior. It is by now well-documented that Russia's is not only a hard authoritarian regime, but a strongly kleptocratic one.[2] As James Sherr has explained, the character of the regime has strong foreign policy implications:

> An overarching aim can be ascribed to Russia: the creation of an international environment conducive to the maintenance of its system of governance at home … The problem now, as in the Soviet past, is that 'national interest' means *regime* interest first and foremost, and any audit of Russian policy that ignores this reality is artificial.[3]

This informs Russia's approach toward the West: Moscow's rivalry with the West is not just a nineteenth century-style geopolitical struggle for influence. Moscow views the West – and particularly the EU and

---

[1] Valentina Pop, "EU Expanding Its 'Sphere of Influence,' Russia Says", EUObserver.com, March 21, 2009. (https://euobserver.com/foreign/27827)

[2] Karen Dawisha, *Putin's Kleptocracy: Who Owns Russia?* , New York: Simon and Schuster, 2014.

[3] James Sherr, *Hard Diplomacy and Soft Coercion: Russia's Influence Abroad*, London: Royal Institute for International Affairs/Chatham House, 2013, p. 96.

NATO as institutions – as a danger not just to its interests, but to the survival of its regime. This is not because Russia fears NATO's military power. It is because of the power of attraction of the normative principles underlying these institutions. As Sherr puts it, "the more the EU's norms and practices gain adherents and traction, the more incongruous Russia's model of governance appears."[4]

As a result, Russian policies actively seek to undermine the attraction of the West internationally. Both to its own public and to the world, Moscow seeks to show western democracies to be decadent and chaotic; to undermine their legitimacy. As author Peter Pomerantsev puts it, the aim is to show that "nothing is true and everything is possible."[5]

These aims are achieved in part through information warfare, including television and news outlets such as RT and Sputnik; but also through direct support for both far-right and far-left political forces in Europe that oppose NATO and EU integration, and support Russian policy goals. Intervention in the U.S. election fulfills the same goal. It is not about supporting one candidate or the other: it is about generating chaos, crippling the functioning of the political system, and undermining the legitimacy of the American system of government. Almost by definition, this means that if Moscow sought to support one particular party or individual *before* an election, it must switch sides and undermine that same person or party *after* the election. This is why, after the 2016 election, the same Russian trolls that are accused of having worked to undermine Hillary Clinton now sought to undermine the legitimacy of Trump's election.

While Western leaders have tended to give Russian leaders the benefit of the doubt, the Russian approach has been the opposite: a fundamental distrust for the intentions of the West. In this sense, like Western leaders, Russian leaders have tended to ascribe their own intentions to their counterparts. Since Russian leaders seek to maximize their power and influence at the expense of the West, they have showed an inclination to assume the west is doing exactly the same. That is why Lavrov termed the EU's rather innocuous Eastern Partnership an attempt to build a Sphere of Influence.

This divergence in political mentality derives, no doubt, from the divergent political culture of Soviet Russia, which framed the worldview of the current leadership crop – itself disproportionally with a past in the security services. Indeed, their approach derives from the Leninist conception of politics as a zero-sum game, defined in terms of who will prevail over whom – summarized in the Russian phrase *"Kto-kogo."* American writer and diplomat Raymond Garthoff has summarized the divergence between this and the western mentality succinctly:

> The cold war was a zero-sum game in which the gains of one side were automatically losses to the other, ruling out genuine compromise, reconciliation, shared interests, and conflict resolution by any other means than prevailing over the other. In Marxist-Leninist terms, this was encapsulated in the phrase *Kto-Kogo?* Who will prevail over whom? In analytical terms, the communist version posited a "correlation of forces" between

---

[4] Sherr, p. 97.
[5] Peter Pomerantsev, *Nothing is True and Everything is Possible: The Surreal Heart of the New Russia*, New York: Public Affairs, 2014.

> adversaries, a version of the balance of power with the important distinction that while the given relationship at any moment would be in flux, the ultimate objective and result would be not an equilibrium balance, but victory for the side that prevailed when the correlation ultimately tipped decisively. This conception was rarely recognized in the west, and when it was it was almost always interpreted in terms of the military balance of forces, which was *not* the Marxist-Leninist conception.[6]

In sum, the West has sought relations with Russia on a win-win basis seeking common interests, but it has tended to misjudge what the Russia leadership's interests are – in part because of a tendency to extrapolate what Russia's interests *should* be if Russia operated as a western country. By contrast, Russia has increasingly seen relations with the West as a zero-sum game, in which it has been Russia's aim to undermine the western-led international order, as well as sow division within western institutions themselves.

This does not mean the West has not made its share of mistakes. The U.S. invasion of Iraq, the recognition of Kosovo's independence, and the Libyan intervention that led to the killing of Muammar Qaddafi can all fairly be criticized for failing to abide by international standards, and of being examples of western unilateralism. The point, however, is that in neither of these situations was the West's aim, let alone its primary objective, to undermine Russian interests. By contrast, Moscow has continuously seized on every western mistake, ascribed the worst of intentions to it, and used it as a precedent to achieve its own unilateral goals at the expense of western interests.

Russia and Ethnonationalist Insurgents

The former Soviet space provides the most overt example of Russian subversion of western interests and international norms, as it is an area where Russia has overt claims to geopolitical domination. Following Vladimir Putin's ascent to power, there was an initial spring in Russia-West relations. Many welcomed a younger, more effective leader who seemed able to put Russia back together. And following the September 11, 2001, terrorist attacks on the United States, Russia immediately seized the opportunity to portray itself as an ally in the fight against terrorism. Yet significant differences between the West and Russia continued to mount in parallel, and were centered on the post-Soviet space, which formed the focus of Putin's policies.

Putin reaped a rapid benefit from his support for the anti-terror coalition: the West, collectively, responded by dropping most of its vocal criticism of Russia's warfare in Chechnya. Seeing Western concessions, Moscow voiced vociferous allegations that both Azerbaijan and Georgia supported Chechen separatists, and went so far as to claim that a thousand Taliban fighters had crossed Azerbaijani and Georgian territory to get to Chechnya. No evidence to corroborate this, or even the

---

[6] Raymond Garthoff, *A Journey through the Cold War: A Memoir of Containment and Coexistence*, Washington: Brookings Institution, 2001, p. 393-4.

presence in Chechnya of such fighters, was ever produced. Still, Moscow followed up by gradually increasing pressure on Georgia. The Kremlin had demanded a right to use Georgian territory against Chechen rebels since 1999. Following 9/11, Moscow sought to apply the doctrine of pre-emptive strike on Georgia's Pankisi gorge, where several thousand Chechens, including several dozen fighters, had sought refuge. Moscow accused Tbilisi of harboring rebels, and threatened to take action to root them out.

The timing of these Russian claims was no accident. In September 2002, the U.S. movement toward military action in Iraq was well under way. At that very moment, in fact on the first anniversary of 9/11, Putin threatened military action against Georgia, thereby trying to link Georgia with international terrorism. Simply put, Putin tried to establish a quid pro quo: if America can attack Iraq, Russia can attack Georgia – irrespective of the polar differences between Saddam Hussein's Iraq and Georgia, a weak but pluralistic and pro-Western republic.

Thankfully, the U.S. did not engage in horse-trading with Russia. Russian intervention was averted by a U.S. Train and Equip Program for the Georgian military, which enabled it to reassert control over the Pankisi gorge in the fall of 2002 – and thus remove the rationale for Moscow's threats. But over the next several years, Moscow gradually stepped up its pressure on Georgia, using what we now call hybrid warfare – a combination of economic warfare, diplomatic pressure and subversion, as well as the manipulation of Georgia' unresolved conflicts. By 2007, the escalation included the use of force against Georgian territory on two occasions, and the escalation to Russia's premeditated invasion of Georgia in 2008. During this invasion, Moscow again took a page from the American playbook, when Sergey Lavrov in a phone conversation with Secretary of State Condoleezza Rice demanded regime change in Georgia. Putin went so far as to explain to French President Nicolas Sarkozy that because the Americans had hung Saddam Hussein, he could hang Georgian President Saakashvili. The operation in Georgia, of course, was a precursor to Russia's military actions in Ukraine six years later.

But even before Ukraine, Moscow moved against other U.S. interests in the post-Soviet space. Its particular focus was Kyrgyzstan, where the U.S. had a military base. The focus on Georgia, Kyrgyzstan and Ukraine is no coincidence: these were the three states that had experience "color revolutions" between 2003 and 2005 – the popular ouster of corrupt and ineffectual governments. These revolutions were welcomed in the United States as a sign of democratic development in the region. But to Russia, they posed a mortal danger: the expansion of successful democratic government along Russia's borders would have endangered the continued dominance of a kleptocratic, authoritarian government over Russia itself. As a result, Moscow decided that the color revolutions had to fail, to ensure that its own regime security stayed intact.

For this purpose, Moscow on one hand backed up authoritarian governments across the region, and instilled in them the fear that Washington was out to overthrow them. On the other, it moved to actively undermine the governments of Georgia, Ukraine, and Kyrgyzstan. In regard to the latter, Moscow actively worked to ensure the removal of the remaining U.S. base in Kyrgyzstan. Bishkek's refusal to follow Moscow's line on this issue led Moscow to support a coup d'état, which brought down the government of Kurmanbek Bakiyev in 2010. The U.S. base was subsequently closed down.

The conflict in Ukraine is, in a way, the consequence and culmination of the Western policy toward Russia in the former Soviet space. Having seen little resistance to its steps to perfect tactics of hybrid warfare against smaller post-Soviet states, there was little to restrain Moscow from taking the plunge in Ukraine in 2014. In this case, Moscow's policies went further than they had previously: instead of supporting existing insurgent elements abroad, Russia now created them *ex nihilo*. There had been no organized insurgent forces countering Ukrainian sovereignty in Crimea or the Donbass. Russia famously annexed Crimea after dispatching "little green men" to the territory; in the Donbass, Russia actively created the militias that would declare the "People's Republic s" of Donetsk and Luhansk by mobilizing, training and arming local Russian nationalist and criminal groupings.

Russia and Islamist Terrorism at Home and Abroad

Russia is often portrayed as an ally in the struggle against Radical Islamic terrorism. Since the rise of the Islamic State several years ago, observers and politicians in both Europe and the United States have increasingly pointed to the need to work with Russia against this common threat – even if this means ignoring or downplaying Russia's territorial grabs in Eastern Europe, or its other efforts to undermine American interests. However, closer examination of Russian policies shows that Moscow has a highly ambiguous relationship to Islamic extremism. When it suits its interests, the Kremlin can crack down on Islamic terrorists. But more often, it appears to view Islamic terrorists as a force to be manipulated to advance its interests and undermine America's. As will be seen, this holds true for Russia's relationship to Islamic extremists both at home and abroad.

Afghanistan

Reports emerged in 2015 of growing Russian contacts with and support for the Taliban insurgency in Afghanistan. In December 2015, President Putin's Special Envoy for Afghanistan openly stated that Russia's Interests in Afghanistan "objectively coincide" with the Taliban.[7] While Moscow claimed that interest was to counter the growing role of ISIS in Afghanistan, a Taliban spokesperson explained the real rationale. Speaking to Reuters, the unnamed "senior Taliban official" explained that the Taliban had been in contact with Russia since 2007, long before ISIS existed. He lamented that these contacts "did not extend beyond 'political and moral support'" but added that "we had a common enemy...we needed support to get rid of the United States and its allies ... Russia wanted all foreign troops to leave Afghanistan as quickly as possible."[8]

This, of course, flies in the face of the notion of Russia as an ally in Afghanistan. Yet that very notion – that Russia backed the U.S. war effort in Afghanistan to begin with – is flawed. In fact, already in the early days of the military campaign against the Taliban, Moscow acted to deny the U.S. the ability to

---

[7] "Russia's Interests in Afghanistan Coincide with Taliban's in Fight against ISIS: Agency Cites Diplomat", *Reuters*, December 23, 2015.

[8] "Ties between Russia and the Taliban Worry Afghan, U.S. Officials", *Reuters*, December 7, 2016.

achieve its goals. President Putin called every head of state in Central Asia and informed them that they would need to seek Russian permission for any cooperative venture with the United States. After Uzbek president Islam Karimov ignored this piece of Russian advice, other regional leaders followed suit and made bilateral agreements with the U.S. anyway. But Russia's efforts in Afghanistan did not stop here, because Moscow inserted itself directly into the war in Afghanistan. Whereas Russia had no role in the military effort to overthrow the Taliban, it capitalized on its long-standing links with the Northern Alliance, particularly its leader Mohammed Fahim, and implemented what Frederick Starr has termed "an aggressive plan to preempt America's growing role in Afghanistan."[9] When the Taliban retreated from Kabul in November 2001, President Bush and other American officials personally pleaded with the Northern Alliance leaders not to take the city, since that would prevent the emergence of a broad-based government that included proper representation of the majority Pashtun population, from which the Taliban had sprung.[10] President Putin, by contrast, urged Fahim to do exactly that, and provided both international cover as well as twelve transport planes full of Russian troops and equipment to back up Fahim. As a result, the Northern Alliance established itself as the dominant force in Kabul, and essentially hijacked the new Afghan government. This played an important role in generating Pashtun resentment at their marginalization from power, and in turn provided fuel to the Taliban insurgency. As Starr concludes, "to none of this did the U.S. administration raise the slightest public objection. If there were private objections they were simply dismissed."[11]

Similarly, restrictions on transit through Russia forced the U.S. to rely almost entirely on the air corridor across Georgia and Azerbaijan for logistical support to the operation in Afghanistan. Yet when time came for Obama's "surge" in Afghanistan, the U.S., building on the "Reset", once again focused on Russia as the main conduit for what would be called the "Northern Distribution Network". We now know, thanks to the above-mentioned Taliban commander, that Moscow was simultaneously tramping up its relationship with the Taliban to undermine America's war effort in Afghanistan. More recently, U.S. military officials have confirmed that Moscow is not only supporting the Taliban politically, sending weapons to support the extremist fighting force that is killing American soldiers and working to undermine U.S. efforts to turn Afghanistan into a secure country.[12]

Chechnya

Between the mid-1990s and the early 2000s, the conflict in Chechnya morphed from a contained, nationalist rebellion to a sprawling jihadi insurgency. Counterintuitively as it may seem, Russian policies have contributed directly to this development. In a parallel to the Bosnian conflict, Russian rhetoric mirrored that of the Serbs: against western criticism of Russia's human rights record in Chechnya,

---

[9] S. Frederick Starr, "Russia's Ominous Afghan Gambit", *Wall Street Journal*, December 11, 2001.
[10] Tony Karon, "Can the Northern Alliance Control Kabul?", *Time*, November 12, 2001.
(http://content.time.com/time/nation/article/0,8599,184221,00.html)
[11] Starr, "Russia's Ominous Afghan Gambit."
[12] "Russia is Sending weapons to Taliban, Top U.S. General Confirms", *Washington Post*, April 24, 2017.
(https://www.washingtonpost.com/news/checkpoint/wp/2017/04/24/russia-is-sending-weapons-to-taliban-top-u-s-general-confirms/?utm_term=.bef13e7c36e6)

Moscow painted itself as a misunderstood defender of Europe against the threat of Islamic radicalism, the "green wave." But more than just arguing for their case, Russian officials actively worked to make the reality of the conflict conform to their vision of it. Thus, there was a remarkable pattern in Russia's priorities during the second Chechen war, from 1999-2003: it prioritized targeting the nationalist Chechen leadership rather than the jihadi elements within the insurgency. Therefore, on the battlefield, Russia targeted field commanders like Ruslan Gelayev, as well as Chechen President Aslan Maskhadov, whom Russian forces killed in March 2005. On the diplomatic front, Russian diplomats and lawyers furiously prosecuted and sought the extradition of secular leaders like Akhmed Zakayev from the United Kingdom and Ilyas Akhmadov from the United States. By comparison, Islamist Chechen leaders have fared much better. Among exiles, Movladi Udugov remains alive, among the few remaining members of the first generation of Chechen leaders to survive. Zelimkhan Yandarbiyev was killed in Qatar by Russian agents, but only in 2004.

In fact, there is considerable evidence tying some of the most virulent Jihadis in the North Caucasian resistance to the Russian intelligence services. This is the case for Shamil Basayev, publicly Russia's public enemy number one before his death in 2006, which was likely caused by an accidental detonation of explosives in a truck he was driving.[13] Allegations of Basayev's GRU connections during the Georgia-Abkhaz war are well-established. In the period between the two Chechen wars, Basayev played an important role in undermining the rule of the nationalist Chechen President, Aslan Maskhadov. Together with the Jordanian-born jihadi Samir Saleh Abdullah Al-Khattab, Basayev had established an "Islamic Brigade" in southeastern Chechnya that attracted foreign fighters, and openly challenged the authority of Maskhadov's government. While Maskhadov sought a dialogue with Moscow to jointly deal with this challenge, it is by now clear that Moscow had no objection to the rise of the radical faction within Chechnya. Indeed, there is considerable evidence that Moscow actively enticed Basayev and Khattab to engage in their ill-fated invasion of neighboring Dagestan in August 1999, which provided Moscow with a rationale for restarting the war in Chechnya that fall. That local conflict – and the very murky apartment bombings in Moscow the next month, both of which led to the second Chechen war – was an inextricable part of the rise of Vladimir Putin to power.

Both Russian and Western investigative reporters and scholars have unearthed considerable evidence that the "family" – i.e. the oligarchs surrounding Boris Yeltsin – used their relationship with Basayev to nudge the Chechen extremists toward their invasion of Dagestan. Several – including respected Hoover Institution scholar John Dunlop – corroborate the reporting that French and Israeli intelligence confirmed that high-level Russian officials met with Basayev in a villa in southern France owned by arms dealer Adnan Khashoggi in July 1999, a month before the incursion into Dagestan.[14] Not staying at that, American scholar David Satter documents how Russian "internal forces assigned to guard the border

---

[13] "Basayev's Death May Have Been an Accident," Prague Watchdog, July 10, 2006; "Basayev Didn't Save Face," Kommersant, July 11, 2006, available from www.kommersant.com/page. asp?idr=527&id=689111.

[14] John Dunlop, *The Moscow Bombings of September 1999: Examinations of Russian Terrorist Attacks at the Onset of Vladimir Putin's Rule*, Stuttgart: Ibidem-Verlag, 2012, 70– 71. Also Boris Kagarlitskiy, "S terroristami ne razgovarivaem: No pomogayem? [We do not negotiate with terrorists. But do we help them?]," *Novaya Gazeta*, January 24, 2000; Karen Dawisha, *Putin's Kleptocracy: Who Owns Russia?* , New York: Simon and Schuster, 2014, p. 200.

[between Chechnya and Dagestan] had been withdrawn shortly before the Chechens invaded, so the force led by Basayev and Khattab entered Dagestan without resistance."[15] The point here is not to ascertain whether Basayev was a fully-controlled Russian operative, or whether the relationship was more *ad hoc:* the point is that leading figures in Moscow actively participated in the manipulation of Islamic terrorists on Russia's own territory.

Equally clear evidence is available in the case of Arbi Barayev, one of the most viciously militant as well as most criminalized of Chechnya's warlords. Barayev was one of the key forces seeking to undermine Maskhadov's leadership in the interwar era; it was his group that kidnapped and beheaded foreign telecommunications workers in 1998, effectively forcing out the small international presence in Chechnya. Similarly Barayev's forces engaged in firefights with Maskhadov's troops in 1998. Following the renewed warfare, Barayev lived freely in the town of Alkhan-Kala, under Russian control, until his death in 2001—despite the fact that he was responsible for gruesome, video-recorded murders of captive Russian servicemen that would preview the tactics of Abu Musab al-Zarqawi and ISIS. As several observers have noted, his opulent residence was only a few miles away from a Russian checkpoint near his native Alkhan-Kala, while his car had an FSB identification which allowed him to race through Russian checkpoints.[16] Tellingly, Barayev was killed by a GRU hit squad only after the FSB's then-head of counterterrorism, General Ugryumov, had died. The apparent conclusion was that Ugryumov provided a cover for Barayev, and the former's death made it possible for the GRU to take Barayev out.

Given the nature of the Chechen conflict, evidence can at best be inconclusive. But circumstantial evidence suggests two things: First, that during the second war there was no clear and unified chain of command Detachments of the Russian army, GRU, FSB, and Ministry of Interior played different roles in the conflict, roles that were poorly coordinated; moreover, they each appeared to keep ties with some Chechen commanders, while combating others. Second, the policies of the Russian leadership itself contributed to change the nature of the conflict from a nationalist rebellion to one where the enemy was Islamic jihadis. While this is likely in the long run to be of greater danger to Russia, it did succeed in making the conflict fit into Moscow's desired narrative. Maskhadov and the Chechen nationalist leadership was respected in Western circles, being granted meetings with Western officials and maintaining strong support among Western media, civil society, and human rights organizations. The jihadi elements, needless to say, did not and do not enjoy this status. By targeting the nationalist faction and covertly protecting or encouraging the jihadi forces in the North Caucasus, Moscow shoehorned the conflict into the template of a "war on terror".

Syria: Applying the Chechnya Model

---

[15] David Satter, *Darkness at Dawn: The Rise of the Russian Criminal State*, New Haven: Yale University Press, 2003, p. 64.
[16] Sanobar Shermatova, "The Secret War between Russian Intelligence Agencies," Moscow News, August 8, 2000. Also see Khassan Baiev, Nicholas Daniloff, and Ruth Daniloff, *The Oath: A Surgeon Under Fire*, New York: Walker & Company, 2004.

In Syria, the U.S. went to great lengths to solicit Russian cooperation – so much so that the U.S. Secretary of State, John F. Kerry, accepted to wait for three hours for a meeting with Vladimir Putin.[17] While the U.S. sought the removal of Syrian President Bashar al-Assad, Russia was the strongest supporter of the Assad regime on the international scene. To this effect, Russia found a perfect opportunity to intervene in fall 2013, when President Obama appeared on the path to begin military action in Syria but reneged on his earlier stated "red line" that would trigger U.S. intervention if the Assad regime used chemical weapons. This led to a serious loss of credibility for the American president, and a marked return of Russia as a power player in the Middle East.

Indeed, it is against this background that Russia's military deployment in Syria should be seen. The Russian leadership concluded that the U.S. did not have a Syria strategy, and that Turkey, which wanted to intervene to topple Assad, would not move without the U.S. in lockstep. As George Friedman has argued, Russia's intervention in "Syria was not about Syria". It was motivated in part by saving the Assad regime, but equally by "showing that it could" to the U.S. and to a domestic audience following being bogged down in Ukraine:

> It demonstrated to the United States that it had the ability and will to intrude into areas that the United States regarded as its own area of operations. It changed the perception of Russia as a declining power unable to control Ukraine, to a significant global force. Whether this was true was less important – it needed to appear to be true.[18]

This is relevant to a discussion of Russia's role as a counter-terrorist partner because Moscow applied a number of lessons from its war in Chechnya. As noted, during the second Chechen war Moscow applied most of its resources to defeat the nationalist, moderate elements of the Chechen resistance – rather than targeting the radical Islamist elements. Similarly in Syria, the Russian intention all along was to leave a choice between the Assad regime and ISIS, a situation in which western leaders would grudgingly accept the Syrian regime as the lesser evil.[19] It is precisely for this reason that the Russian bombing overwhelmingly targeted not ISIS, but Syrian opposition groups aligned with the United States, Turkey, or other Arab allies. In other words, whereas the U.S. and Europe ideally want to defeat ISIS and ease Assad out of power in a negotiated settlement, Russia wants to eliminate any military force on the ground that could help achieve that objective. The goals of the West and Russia are simply incompatible. Yet in spite of this, the U.S. and Europe continue to seek ways to convince Moscow to cooperate on ways to resolve the Syrian conflict.

---

[17] Shaun Walker, "Russia and US agree to hold Syrian peace conference", *Independent*, 7 May 2013. (http://www.independent.co.uk/news/world/middle-east/russia-and-us-agree-to-hold-syrian-peace-conference-8606793.html), "Russia and US agree to hold Syrian peace conference", *Independent*, 7 May. (http://www.independent.co.uk/news/world/middle-east/russia-and-us-agree-to-hold-syrian-peace-conference-8606793.html)

[18] George Friedman, "Why Putin Went into Syria", *Geopolitical Futures*, March 15, 2016. (https://geopoliticalfutures.com/why-putin-went-into-syria/)

[19] Andrew Foxall, "To See Syria's Future, Look at Chechnya", *American Interest*, December 4, 2015.. (http://www.the-american-interest.com/2015/12/04/to-see-syrias-future-look-at-chechnya/)

Conclusions

Russia's behavior internationally as well as domestically suggests that is attitude toward insurgency and terrorism conflict fundamentally with the United States. For Russia, insurgency and terrorism are instruments of hybrid warfare that may at times be fought, and at times supported, depending on what suits the perceived national and regime interests of the Kremlin. Furthermore, the record suggests that Russia views these issues in the light of a competition for influence in the world, in which Moscow knows it cannot meet the United States eye to eye. To maximize its influence, therefore, the Kremlin sees insurgency and terrorism as forces to be manipulated for the purpose of weakening America's position in the world, undermine U.S. allies, and maximize Russian influence in word affairs. This is a matter the United States cannot fail to respond to. While the United States may need to work with Russia on a case-by-case basis, it must understand that Russia views all its instruments of statecraft as interconnected, serving a common purpose; and that Russia's aims are seldom, if ever, compatible with those of the United States – simple because the reduction of American and Western influence in the world remain a key goal of Russian policy.

Mr. POE. Thank you, Dr. Cornell.

The Chair recognizes Mr. Saradzhyan for his 5-minute opening statement. You may proceed.

STATEMENT OF MR. SIMON SARADZHYAN, DIRECTOR OF THE RUSSIA MATTERS PROJECT, ASSISTANT DIRECTOR OF U.S.-RUSSIA INITIATIVE TO PREVENT NUCLEAR TERRORISM, BELFER CENTER FOR SCIENCE AND INTERNATIONAL AFFAIRS, HARVARD KENNEDY SCHOOL

Mr. SARADZHYAN. Thank you, distinguished members of the committee, for inviting me to give my testimony, which reflects my personal views only, rather than the views of the organizations I work for.

I have been asked to answer five questions. The first one is, can Russia be an effective counterterrorism partner for the United States? In my view, yes, Russia can be an effective counterterrorism partner for the United States in theory.

Why I think so—as some of you have mentioned, the U.S. and Russia do share common interests in reducing the threat posed by Islamist militant nonstate actors that seek to build caliphates, or a global caliphate, in the Middle East and in parts of the post-Soviet neighborhood.

The U.S. and Russia also share a vital national interest in preventing any nonstate actors, including these Islamist groups, from acquiring nuclear weapons. And we know that both al-Qaeda and the Islamic State have displayed practical interest in getting those nuclear weapons.

At the same time, as we know, the events, the conflict in Ukraine, the conflict in Syria, Russia's alleged meddling in the U.S. elections, have imposed constraints on realizing the potential for this cooperation. Therefore, I am skeptical that in the short-to-medium future the two countries would act on their joint common interests in countering such groups.

The second question I have been asked, what is actually Russia's counterterrorism strategy? I would say Russia's counterterrorism strategy employs both forceful and nonforceful elements.

The forceful elements are best displayed in Russia's North Caucasus, from which more than 80 percent of attacks against targets in Russia have originated, according to the global database on terrorism maintained by the University of Maryland.

At the same time, we have seen in the past few years that the threat of militant Islamism has proliferated to some of the other regions of Russia, including Volga region, the Urals, and even Siberia.

So Russia's counterterrorism approach, the forceful component, has been focused on removing the leadership of the groups operating in these regions and also neutralizing members of these groups. In the process of doing so, Russian law enforcement officials have been accused of abuses, including enforced disappearances, extrajudicial killings, and torture.

In my view, and in the view of scholars who study Russia's North Caucasus, these are some of the root causes that fuel insurgency and terrorism in Russia.

At the same time, there is a nonforceful component, and that has been displayed in the North Caucasus, too, where Russian authorities have sought to reduce at least some of the disengagement costs for the terrorists and rebels who have not committed grave offenses. However, these efforts fall short of addressing all the root causes behind an insurgency.

The same can be said about Russia's counterterrorism strategy abroad, mainly in Syria, where it is mostly a military operation, but where some special forces operate against certain leaders of the insurgency. But here, the accent on forceful methods has been much more emphasized, and, again, NGOs have accused Russian aircraft of indiscriminate bombing that again fuels grievances and can contribute to the rise of insurgency.

The third question I have been asked to answer was, what is Russia's military engagement in the Middle East? Again, it is mostly focused on Syria. And here I would say Russia's vital interest in Syria is not Assad, per se, but Syria has been Russia's ally for many years. So preserving Syria as an ally is an important interest.

At the same time, Russia also wants to make sure that Syria does not become a haven for terrorist groups that can attack Russia, given the fact that there are about 5,000 nationals of Russia and about 4,000 nationals of Central Asia in the ranks of terrorism and insurgency groups in Iraq and Syria, according to Russia's own estimate. So neutralizing these individuals and making sure they do not pose a threat to Russia is a vital interest of Russia.

The fourth question I have been asked to answer is, what are the current terrorist threats within Russia? As I have said, these are posed by Islamist groups, but also there is a smaller number of threats posed by individual avengers who use terrorist methods, and also by ethnic Russian ultranationalists who have used terrorist methods to attack foreigners, but also some of Russia's own government officials, including judges.

We have seen the surge in the number of terrorist attacks in Russia in 2010. Since then it has been declining.

And finally, the final question I have been asked to answer is: How do Russian counterterrorism and military operations impact the terror threat worldwide?

I would say the impact in the North Caucasus is of dual nature. On one hand, the threat of terrorism is being reduced because leaders have been taken out and members of an insurgency have been arrested. But on the other hand, the abuses I have described fuel some of the grievances and recruit fertile ground for recruitment of new members into existing insurgency networks. The same can be said about Russia's operations abroad.

Thank you.

[The prepared statement of Mr. Saradzhyan follows:]

Testimony by Simon Saradzhyan[1] at hearing entitled "Russia: Counterterrorism Partner or Fanning the Flames" and held by the House Committee on Foreign Affairs on Nov. 7, 2017.

Allow me to begin by saying that I am delivering this testimony in my personal capacity; it does not represent the views and positions of Harvard Kennedy School or its Belfer Center for Science and International Affairs or of the Russia Matters Project, and it is based solely on open sources. This testimony seeks to answer the following questions that I have been asked to address: (1) Can Russia be an effective counterterrorism partner for the United States? (2) What is Russia's counterterrorism strategy? (3) What is Russia's military engagement in the Middle East? (4) What are the current terrorist threats within Russia? (5) How do Russian counter-terrorism and military operations impact the terror threat worldwide?

Question 1. Can Russia be an effective counterterrorism partner for the United States?
Answer 1. Theoretically, Russia can be an effective partner for the U.S. in countering non-state actors that espouse use of violence in their efforts to establish Islamist rule within and without the greater Middle East (GME) and the post-Soviet neighborhood and that are willing to use force against stakeholders that oppose their plans. The U.S. and Russia are both such stakeholders and they share a very important interest in preventing these non-state actors from overthrowing secular regimes in the GME and from targeting Washington, Moscow and their respective allies in violent campaigns using terrorist strategy. GME-based Islamist non-state actors that have targeted both the U.S. and Russia, as well as their allies, and continue to do so include al-Qaeda and Islamic State. The United States' and Russia's shared interest in minimizing and/or dismantling threats posted by AQ, IS and other violent non-state actors have made it possible to preserve some level of U.S.-Russian counterterrorism coordination and intelligence sharing despite the sharp deterioration in the bilateral relationship caused by the conflict in Ukraine and other factors. However, the current level of U.S.-Russian CT interaction appear to be a far cry from earlier periods—specifically, in the wake of the 9/11 attacks and then during the presidencies of Barack Obama and Dmitry Medvedev when U.S. and Russian government agencies responsible for counterterrorism actively worked with each other in the framework of the bilateral presidential commission to tame the international challenges posed by groups employing terrorism to attain political goals.

I have access only to open sources, so I do not have the full picture, but judging by these sources, my supposition is that some of the U.S.-Russian dialogue on counterterrorism may have been revived since Donald Trump's arrival at the White House. Three recent events and statements attest to this: the trip that CIA director Mike Pompeo reportedly made to Moscow in May[2]; the recent claim by the director of Russia's Federal Security Service, Alexander Bortnikov, that the

---

[1] The author of this statement is a Russian citizen and a permanent U.S. resident. He is the director of the Russia Matters Project at Harvard Kennedy School's Belfer Center for Science and International Affairs and assistant director of the center's U.S.-Russia Initiative to Prevent Nuclear Terrorism.
[2] Damien Sharkov, "Mike Pompeo's Moscow Visit: What the CIA Director May Have Discussed In Russia," Newsweek, August 25, 2017. Available at http://www.newsweek.com/mike-pompeo-moscow-visit-what-cia-director-may-have-discussed-russia-655241

FBI and CIA sent officials "at the level of department heads" to an annual gathering of security service chiefs in Russia in October[3]; and Russian President Vladimir Putin's October 2017 statement that the U.S. and Russia "have a dialogue at the working level, at the level of special services, the Defense Ministry and the Foreign Ministry, almost on a weekly basis" on the Syrian issue.[4] Also, while U.S. laws prohibit the U.S. military from cooperating with the Russian military on Syria, the two sides are actively engaged in the so-called deconflicting of their respective campaigns in Syria, which is very important because it helps reduce the chances of Washington and Moscow stumbling into an accidental conflict.

Russia certainly has the capacity to become an effective counterterrorism partner to the U.S. in theory. It traditionally boasts formidable intelligence capabilities in the greater Middle East, as well as in the post-Soviet neighborhood, from which some of the international threats of terrorist attacks are currently emanating. Greater sharing of such intelligence by Russia would benefit the United States. Russia's security and defense agencies also play an important role in deterring and targeting terrorist groups operating within the former Soviet Union, in such areas as Russia's own North Caucasus, and in the Central Asian republics. As we know, natives of these regions have staged attacks against the U.S., Russia and their allies in the past and, unfortunately, there's a significant possibility that such attacks will continue.

Whether Russia's theoretical ability to become an effective CT partner for the U.S. will become reality depends on a number of factors, most of which have little to do with terrorism per se, but a lot to do with shaping the general political relationship between the two countries. One such factor is the outcome of the multiple investigations into Russia's alleged meddling in the U.S. elections pursued by special counsel Robert Mueller and Congressional committees. Another factor is the Ukraine conflict, which, if unresolved, will continue to limit America's willingness to cooperate with Russia. Yet another factor is the resolution of the conflict in Syria, which the U.S. and Russia continue to disagree about, although these differences are not as stark as in the case of the Ukraine conflict. The U.S. has also introduced a number of punitive measures against Russia over its conduct in Ukraine and Syria, as well as its alleged interference in the U.S. presidential election, that reduce the possibilities for U.S.-Russian counterterrorism cooperation. These measures include:

- The National Defense Authorization Act for Fiscal Year 2017 prohibits any U.S. funds "from being used for bilateral military-to-military cooperation between the governments of the United States and Russia until DOD certifies to Congress that Russia: (1) has ceased its occupation of Ukrainian territory and its aggressive activities that threaten the sovereignty and territorial integrity of Ukraine and members of the North Atlantic Treaty Organization; and (2) is abiding by the terms of and taking steps in support of the Minsk Protocols regarding a ceasefire in eastern Ukraine. Specifies exceptions and permits a waiver for national security."
- The Countering America's Adversaries Through Sanctions Act of 2017 bars any "significant transaction with a person that is part of, or operates for or on behalf of, the

---

[3] Russia in Review, Sept. 29-Oct. 6, 2017. Available at https://www.russiamatters.org/news/russia-review/russia-review-sept-29-oct-6-2017
[4] "Meeting of the Valdai International Discussion Club," Kremlin.ru, October 18, 2017. Available at http://en.kremlin.ru/events/president/news/55882

defense or intelligence sectors of the Government of the Russian Federation, including the Main Intelligence Agency of the General Staff of the Armed Forces of the Russian Federation or the Federal Security Service of the Russian Federation."[5]

U.S. President Trump has repeatedly expressed interest in having the U.S. cooperate with Russia on countering terrorist threats and he may discuss this issue when he meets Vladimir Putin on the sidelines of the Asia-Pacific Economic Cooperation summit that is to take place in Vietnam on November 8-10. However, given the aforementioned constraints, it is difficult to imagine a qualitative improvement in U.S.-Russian counterterrorism cooperation unless there's significant progress on implementing the Minsk-2 accords and unless the ongoing investigations fail to produce any significant evidence of Russian attempts to influence the outcome of the 2016 elections.[6] Moreover, even if progress is achieved both on Ukraine and Syria, it remains unclear whether and which of the U.S. sanctions on Russian government agencies would be lifted.

Question 2. What is Russia's counterterrorism strategy?
Answer 2: The Russian government's counterterrorism strategy employs violent and non-violent means both within Russia and abroad to attain the primary goal of reducing the threat of major and/or repeated terrorist attacks or the outbreak of insurgency targeting Russia or threatening regime change in countries allied with Russia.

Internally, Russian authorities have traditionally focused on using force to degrade various groups based in the North Caucasus and engaged in anti-state violence irrespective of whether these groups employ terrorist or guerilla strategies in their violent campaigns. More recently Russian authorities have also had to deal with the proliferation of militant Islamist networks to other Russian regions, including the Volga, the Urals and Siberia. Again, the response to this proliferation has a robust forceful component. At the same time, Russian authorities have been trying to apply non-forceful methods of countering political violence in individual provinces of Russia. For instance, Russian authorities have tried to lower disengagement costs for those engaged in political violence by promising amnesty or lesser charges to those who agree to disengage before a certain deadline. Such amnesty campaigns have taken place, with varying degree of success, in Chechnya, Dagestan and Ingushetia and other provinces of Russia's North Caucasus.[7] Russian authorities have also occasionally turned a blind eye to those domestic

---

[5] Some of these punitive measures were originally imposed by President Obama in late 2016 in response to Russia's alleged interference in the presidential election. Congress voted to approve the sanctions, as part of the larger Countering America's Adversaries through Sanctions Act in July 2017 and President Trump then signed this act into law in August 2017. In compliance with this law the Trump administration unveiled a list of Russian entities with which significant transactions are prohibited. In addition to the Federal Security Service (FSB), Foreign Intelligence Service (SVR) and Main Intelligence Directorate of the General Staff of the Russian Armed Forces (GRU), the following three Russian entities are included in the list and identified as part of the Intelligence Sector of the Government of the Russian Federation: Autonomous Noncommercial Professional Organization/Professional Association of Designers of Data Processing (ANO PO KSI), Special Technology Center and Zorsecurity.
[6] In my view, while the recent discussion of introducing international peacekeepers into the conflict zone in eastern Ukraine is a welcome development, the implementation of Minsk-2 remains unlikely in the near to medium term. In contrast, I am slightly more optimistic about the possibility of a political resolution of the Syrian conflict.
[7] One of the larger amnesties for rebels was introduced by the State Duma, Russia's lower house of parliament, in July 2006 and it applied to those who committed minor crimes as members of so-called "illegal armed formations"

terrorists and guerillas who have expressed interest in relocating to Syria and Iraq in hopes of joining the ranks of those fighting for the Islamic State or al-Qaeda or other terrorist and guerilla groups operating in these countries, according to reports in Russia's investigative Novaya Gazeta weekly[8] and other Russian media. Russian authorities have denied these reports.

It should be noted that Russian leaders publicly profess an understanding that at least some political violence is partially driven by the ills of a given society. President Vladimir Putin, for instance, recently claimed that a lack of education is among the factors that fuel terrorism. Hence, when assessing the prospects of an end to the Syrian conflict, Putin noted in his October remarks at the Valdai Club: "There is every reason to believe—I will put it cautiously—that we will finish off the terrorists in the short term, but that is no cause for joy, [or] for saying that terrorism is over and done with. Because, first, terrorism as a phenomenon is deeply rooted—it is rooted in the injustice of today's world, the raw deal that many nations and ethnic and religious groups get, and the lack of comprehensive education in entire countries across the world. The lack of a normal, proper, basic education is fertile soil for terrorism." [9]

However, there are other, more influential factors that, in my view, are not always fully addressed in Russia's counterterrorism approach, although they have been identified by scholars of political violence as either directly causing "men to rebel" or facilitating such rebellions. These factors include abuses committed by individual representatives of the Russian authorities. There is no shortage of scholars studying the North Caucasus who believe that serious abuses of local residents by certain representatives of the authorities in the region have played an important role in fuelling political violence in Russia; these include: Domitilla Sagramoso,[10] John O'Loughlin,[11] Brian Taylor,[12] Neil Bowie,[13] Emil Souleimanov, Huseyn Aliyev,[14] Jean-François Ratelle,[15] Robert Ware and Enver Kisriev.[16]

---

in Dagestan, Ingushetia, Kabardino-Balkaria, Karachaevo-Cherkessia, North Ossetia, Chechnya and Stavropolsky Krai in 1999-2006.

[8] Elena Milashina, "Khalifat? Primanka dlya Durakov!" Novaya Gazeta July 28, 2015. Available at https://www.novayagazeta.ru/articles/2015/07/29/65056-171-halifat-primanka-dlya-durakov-187

[9] "Meeting of the Valdai International Discussion Club," Kremlin.ru, October 18, 2017. Available at http://en.kremlin.ru/events/president/news/55882

10 Sagramoso, Domitilla. "The Radicalisation of Islamic Salafi Jamaats in the North Caucasus: Moving Closer to the Global Jihadist Movement?." Europe-Asia Studies 64, no. 3 (2012): 561-595.

11 O'Loughlin, John, Edward C. Holland, and Frank Witmer. "The Changing Geography of Violence in Russia's North Caucasus, 1999-2011: Regional Trends and Local Dynamics in Dagestan, Ingushetia, and Kabardino-Balkaria." Eurasian Geography and Economics 52.5 (2011): 596-630.

12 Taylor, Brian D. "Putin's 'Historic Mission': State-Building and the Power Ministries in the North Caucasus." Problems of Post-Communism 54, no. 6 (2007): 3-16.

13 Bowie, Neil G., "Trends in the Use of Terror by States since the End of the Cold War," in State Terrorism and Human Rights: International Responses since the End of the Cold War, ed. Duncan, Gullian, Orla Lynch, Gilbert Ramsay, Alison M.S. Watson, (London, UK: Routledge, 2013), 47.

14 Souleimanov, Emil, and Huseyn Aliyev. The Individual Disengagement of Avengers, Nationalists, and Jihadists: Why Ex-militants Choose to Abandon Violence in the North Caucasus. Palgrave Macmillan, 2014, 57.

15 Ratelle, Jean-François, and Emil Aslan Souleimanov. "Retaliation in Rebellion: The Missing Link to Explaining Insurgent Violence in Dagestan." Terrorism and Political Violence (2015): 1-20.

16 Ware, Robert Bruce, and Enver Kisriev. Dagestan: Russian Hegemony and Islamic Resistance in the North Caucasus: Russian Hegemony and Islamic Resistance in the North Caucasus (p. 190). Taylor and Francis. Kindle Edition.

Externally, Russia has also focused its counterterrorism strategy on the employment of both violent and non-violent means to attain the following ends: (1) assisting friendly regimes in preventing the emergence of safe havens for groups that are hostile to Russia and eliminating established safe havens; (2) preventing the overthrow of these regimes by such groups or organizations; (3) eliminating nationals of post-Soviet states that have joined such groups; (4) eliminating leading figures in Russia's domestic insurgency and terrorism who have left Russia but continued to support political violence in Russia. As the Syrian conflict demonstrates, Russia uses mostly military means to attain these and other goals, but Russian leaders also maintain that they realize that a lasting solution can be attained only if (a) political compromise is reached and (b) factors that either directly cause or facilitate political violence in Syria are addressed.[17]

Question 3: What is Russia's military engagement in the Middle East?
Answer 3: Russia's military engagement in the Middle East is first and foremost focused on Syria. In my view, which I outlined in November 2015,[18] the initial minimal objectives of Russia's military engagement in Syria were: (1) to prevent Assad's government from losing control over the remaining part of Syria and from being ousted from power; (2) to bleed Islamic State, al-Qaeda and other non-state actors that have nationals of post-Soviet republics in their ranks and/or which are a threat to security for Russia and its allies; (3) to maintain control of Russia's military facilities in Syria; (4) to prevent Syria from becoming a failed, "terrorist" state that would be run by the likes of IS and play host to non-state actors hostile to Russia; and (5) to gain leverage vis-à-vis the West that can be used in resolving the Ukraine crisis. One could say today that all of these objectives, except for the last one, have been accomplished. The medium- and longer-term objectives of Russia's military engagement in Syria included: (6) to complete roll-back of IS, AQ, etc. in Syria including the "neutralization" of Russian nationals in their ranks, and achieve political resolution of the conflict; (7) to preserve access of Russian companies to Syria's market to ensure that the country continues to buy Russian-made arms and machinery; (8) to ensure that Russia's reputation as a reliable protector of its allies (in the eyes of the latter) is maintained; and (9) to ensure that the example of Syria reaffirms Russia's claim to having a say in major decisions on the global scene in places where Russia plays what its foreign policy doctrine defines as a "balancing role," including the Middle East. One could say that Russia has made significant progress in achieving these four longer-term goals, which advance a number of Russia's national interests that are at stake in Syria (see chart below).

Russia's vital national interests at stake in Syria	
Interest	**Factors that can impact Russia's interest**

---

[17]In his remarks at last month's Valdai Club meeting, Putin praised international efforts to encourage moderate opposition groups and Assad's government to reach a political resolution of the conflict in Syria that would involve drafting a new constitution. He also spoke in favor of addressing some of the factors that he thinks had fueled the surge in political violence there, such as lack of education. "Meeting of the Valdai International Discussion Club," Kremlin.ru, October 18, 2017. Available at http://en.kremlin.ru/events/president/news/55882

[18] Saradzhyan, Simon. "Russia's Actions in Syria: Underlying Interests and Policy Objectives." Presentation at Harvard University's Davis Center for Russian and Eurasian Studies, November 16, 2015. Available at https://www.belfercenter.org/publication/russias-actions-syria-underlying-interests-and-policy-objectives

1. Prevent, deter and reduce threats of secession from Russia, insurgency within Russia or in areas adjacent to Russia and armed conflicts waged against Russia, its allies or in the vicinity of Russian frontiers;	Threat of "export" of insurgency from Syria to Russia: • Long-time ties between al-Qaeda and North Caucasus insurgency; • IS has established a "vilayat" in Russia; • Thousands of nationals of post-Soviet states fighting in ranks of IS, AQ and other groups in Iraq and Syria.
2. Prevent emergence of hostile individual or collective regional hegemonies or failed states on Russian borders; ensure Russia is surrounded by friendly states among which Russia can play a lead role and cooperation with which can lead it to thrive;	Syria as failed state with Central Asian republics among the potential next targets for emboldened architects of the "Islamic State."
3. Establish and maintain productive relations, upon which Russian national interests hinge to a significant extent, with core European Union members, the United States and China;	Russia's military campaign in Syria was for some time seen as an opportunity for Moscow to repair relations with the West, but that opportunity failed to materialize.
4. Ensure the viability and stability of major markets/flows of Russian exports and imports;	Plans for Iran-Iraq-Syria and Qatar-Turkey pipelines?
5. Ensure steady development and diversification of the Russian economy and its integration into global markets;	Syria is a traditional buyer of Russian arms; not too many countries buy Russian machinery, but Syria does.
6. Prevent neighboring nations from acquiring nuclear arms and their long-range delivery systems on Russian borders; secure nuclear weapons and materials;	Both IS and al-Qaeda have displayed practical interest in acquiring nuclear weapons.
7. Prevent large-scale or sustained terrorist attacks on Russia;	Both IS and al-Qaeda have urged their supporters to carry out terrorist attacks against Russia and some have heeded these calls.
8. Ensure Russian allies' survival and their active cooperation with Russia.	Assad's Syria is one of the allies Russia has preserved after disintegration of the Soviet Union.[19]

[19] Saradzhyan, Simon. "Russia's Actions in Syria: Underlying Interests and Policy Objectives." Presentation at Harvard University's Davis Center for Russian and Eurasian Studies, November 16, 2015. Available at https://www.belfercenter.org/publication/russias-actions-syria-underlying-interests-and-policy-objectives

As of last year, Russian Defense Ministry sources estimated the number of Russian soldiers deployed in Syria at the time at 1,600, while then-Deputy Defense Minister Anatoly Antonov (now Russia's ambassador to the U.S.) put the total number of personnel of all of Russia's so-called power agencies that would be rotated in and out of Syria at 25,000.[20] In contrast, the latest edition of The Military Balance, produced by the London-based International Institute for Strategic Studies, put the number of Russian servicemen in Syria at 4,000. This authoritative publication also counted seven tanks, 20 APCs, 25 warplanes, 24 helicopters and two S-400 air defense batteries deployed at various locations, including the air base at Latakia and naval facility at Tartus.[21] While mostly focused on conducting air strikes, providing strategic advice to Syrian commanders and policing lines of separation, Russia's official military grouping there has also reportedly participated in combat, mostly when carrying out reconnaissance, air targeting and special forces missions or defending their positions. In addition to these servicemen, there were also about 2,500 members of Russia's so-called Wagner private military company deployed in Syria as of October 2017, according to Russia's Novaya Gazeta.[22]

Russian leaders have asserted that the official Russian military grouping played a decisive role in the Assad regime's effort, backed by its allies, in rolling back the territorial gains initially made by the Islamic State, al-Qaeda and some of the more moderate foes of the regime. More than 90 percent of Syrian territory has been "liberated from terrorists," according to Putin's October 2017 estimate.[23] According to the Russian Defense Ministry's October 2017 estimate, Russia's armed forces had lost a total of 39 killed in action in Syria and one more serviceman had committed suicide.[24] According to an October 2017 report by Reuters, however, while Russia's official count of KTAs in Syria for 2017 was 16, in reality at least 131 Russian citizens had died in Syria in the first nine months of 2017 alone, including 26 Russian private contractors.[25] The Russian military operations in Syria, which Russian Defense Minister Sergei Shoigu claimed in October to be nearing an end[26] have proved at times to be brutal and indiscriminate, causing many civilian deaths—nearly 4,000 in the first year of the campaign,[27] according to the London-based Syrian Observatory for Human Rights, which continues to blame Russia for scores of civilian deaths with grim regularity.[28]

---

[20] "Ministerstvo Oborony Otsenilo Maksimalnoye Chislo Uchasnikov Operatsii v Syrii," RBC, June 15, 2016. Available at http://www.rbc.ru/politics/15/06/2016/576158899a7947653f16516b

[21] "The Military Balance 2017," International Institute for Strategic Studies, 2017.

[22] "Ikh Prosto Net," Novaya Gazeta, October 8, 2017. Available at
https://www.novayagazeta.ru/articles/2017/10/09/74125-ih-prosto-net

[23] "Vladimir Putin: Ot terroristov svobodno uzhe 90 protsentov Sirii," Kosmomolskaya Pravda, October 26, 2017. Available at https://www.kp.ru/daily/26749/3778421/

[24] "Geroi voyny: poteri Vooruzhennykh sil RF v khode siriyskoy operatsii," TASS, October 10, 2017. Afvailable at http://tass.ru/armiya-i-opk/3445013

[25] "Exclusive: Death certificate offers clues on Russian casualties in Syria," Reuters, October 27, 2017. Available at https://www.reuters.com/article/us-mideast-crisis-russia-syria-casualtie/exclusive-death-certificate-offers-clues-on-russian-casualties-in-syria-idUSKBN1CW1LP

[26] "Rsossiyskoy gruppirovke v Sirii nashli novogo komanduyushchego," RBC, November 2, 2017. Available at http://www.rbc.ru/politics/02/11/2017/59faf43c9a7947fc3cf01c99

[27] Max Rosental. "Russia Has Killed Almost 10,000 Syrians in the Past Year, Says a New Report. That includes nearly 4,000 civilians." Mother Jones, September 20, 2016. Available at
http://www.motherjones.com/politics/2016/09/russia-has-killed-almost-10000-syrians-year-says-new-report/

[28] "How much territory have Russia and Syria recaptured from IS?" BBC, October 27, 2017. Available at http://www.bbc.com/news/world-europe-41766353

Russia has no military groupings in other countries of the Middle East, although it does have five observers serving for the United Nations Truce Supervision Organization in the Middle East and three observers in the U.N. mission in South Sudan, according to The Military Balance 2017.[29] There have also been reports of Russian forces deployed in Egypt to support Libyan military commander Khalifa Haftar, but Russia has denied these.[30] Russia also has successfully negotiated deals to supply arms to such countries in the region as Saudi Arabia, Egypt, Iran, Iraq and Algeria—and some of these supplies should be assumed to be accompanied by the deployment of military trainers. The Middle East has been recently estimated to account for anywhere between 8 percent and 37.5 percent of Russia's annual arms exports.[31]

Question 4: What are the current terrorist threats within Russia?
Answer 4: Russia saw a total of 1,286 terrorism incidents in 2006-2016, according to the University of Maryland's Global Terrorism Database.[32] Of these, Russia's Federal North Caucasus District accounted for 1,093 or 85 percent of all incidents (if counted by location of targets). Of the district's constituent territories, Dagestan saw the greatest number of attacks: 531.Chechnya accounted for 84, Ingushetia for 278, Kabardino-Balkaria for 155, Karachaevo-Cherkessia for 11, North Ossetia for 19, Stavropolsky Krai for 15. It should also be noted that North Caucasus-based groups are likewise responsible for many of the 54 terrorist incidents that occurred in Moscow (47) and St. Petersburg (7) in the 2006-2016 period, though some of those

---

[29] "The Military Balance 2017," International Institute for Strategic Studies, 2017.

[30] "Exclusive: Russia appears to deploy forces in Egypt, eyes on Libya role – sources," Reuters, March 13, 2017. Available at https://www.reuters.com/article/us-usa-russia-libya-exclusive/exclusive-russia-appears-to-deploy-forces-in-egypt-eyes-on-libya-role-sources-idUSKBN16K2RY

[31] Nikolai Kozhanov, "Arms Exports Add to Russia's Tools of Influence in Middle East," Chatham House, July 20, 2016. Available at https://www.chathamhouse.org/expert/comment/arms-exports-add-russia-s-tools-influence-middle-east

[32] The GTD defines terrorism as the threatened or actual use of illegal force and violence by a non-state actor to attain a political, economic, religious or social goal through fear, coercion or intimidation. Available at https://www.start.umd.edu/gtd/

were carried out by nationals of Central Asia, which represents a troubling new trend.

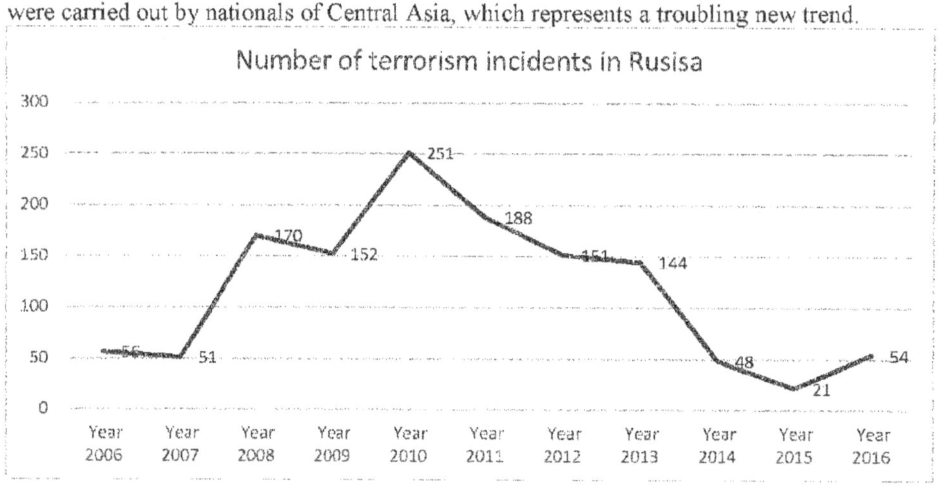

The number of terrorism incidents in Russia began to climb in 2008. This surge peaked in 2010 at 251 and then started to peter out, declining to 21 in 2015, according to GTD. While the reasons for the surge remain to be ascertained, I believe two factors have contributed to the subsequent decline in attacks: Russian government agencies managed to decapitate most of the groups, and some of the fighters chose to leave for the Middle East to join the ranks of local terrorist and insurgency groups in Syria and Iraq, as they believed those groups had a greater chance of creating an independent Sharia state for themselves than did North Caucasus-based groups.

Groups based in the North Caucasus have been most active in employing a strategy of terrorism and guerilla warfare in Russia. Of these groups, those professing a violent interpretation of Salafism and affiliated with the so-called Caucasus Emirate, which has pledged allegiance to al-Qaeda, have recently waned, while groups associated with the so-called Islamic State have gained relative prominence in the past few years. In addition to Islamist insurgents, the North Caucasus has also been home to individual avengers and secular separatists, although the share of the latter in the overall violence has decreased considerably. As stated above, militant Islamist networks have recently proliferated to other Russian regions, including the Volga, the Urals and Siberia, though their share in terrorist attacks remains dwarfed by the attacks that occur in the North Caucasus. For instance, Tatarstan accounted for six attacks in 2006-2016 and Tyumen accounted for two, according to the Global Terrorism Database. In addition to Islamists, separatists and avengers for the abused hailing from Russia's North Caucasus, Russia has also seen a number of terrorist attacks staged by ethnic Russian ultranationalists and avengers (for abuses by law-enforcers), including attacks in which explosives have been employed, but their share in overall terrorist violence has been far smaller than that of North Caucasus-based groups.

It is difficult to project future levels of anti-state violence in Russia. A lot will depend on (a) where the several thousand nationals of Russia and the Central Asian republics believed to be fighting in the ranks of IS, AQ and other groups in Syria and Iraq choose to go next as IS continues to lose territory, (b) what they would choose to do upon relocation and (c) governments' response to their arrival or return. In February 2017 Putin put the number of nationals of post-Soviet states fighting on the rebels' side at 9,000, including 5,000 nationals of Russia.[33] The Soufan Center[34] put the number of Russians who had gone to fight in Syria and Iraq at 3,417, with 400 of them having returned as of March 2016. The center's October 2017 report claimed that the number of Russian nationals who had gone to fight in Syria and Iraq reached 5,000 in July 2017, citing anonymous "informal estimates by security sources." A Kremlin spokesman said Moscow doubts the Soufan Center's estimates.[35]

Question 5: How do Russian counterterrorism and military operations impact the terror threat worldwide?

Answer 5: At least some of the Russian nationals who have left Russia to join the ranks of terrorist and insurgency groups in Syria and Iraq have done so because they thought they stood a greater chance of building a Sharia-ruled state in either of these Arab countries than in Russia where they were actively pursued for either suspected involvement in political violence or association with Salafi groups or both. Therefore, one could say that Russia's ongoing domestic counterterrorism and counter-insurgency campaign has indirectly led to reinforcement of the ranks of jihadists in Syria and Iraq, while reducing the threat in Russia itself. That Syria has not become a permanent haven for IS and AQ groups is in part due to Russia's military campaign there. At the same time, while Russia's military campaign in Syria has helped to degrade both IS and al-Qaeda, the indiscriminate use of non-smart ammunition by Russian aircraft, as asserted by local NGOs[36], has resulted in civilian casualties, quite possibly radicalizing some of the civilians in ways that made them more susceptible to recruitment into terrorist networks.

Conclusion

In conclusion, let me recall Winston Churchill's famous observation: "I cannot forecast to you the action of Russia. It is a riddle, wrapped in a mystery, inside an enigma; but perhaps there is a key. That key is Russian national interest." Today's Russia's leadership continues to be guided by Russia's national interests in their policies and the sphere of counterterrorism is no exception. My reading of the hierarchy of Russia's national interests and America's national interests remains the same, as in my 2015 testimony: Both countries share a vital interest in warding off terrorist threats posed by Islamist groups seeking to build a global caliphate. Whether the existing irritants in the bilateral relationship will continue to constrain cooperation on this vital common interest remains to be seen, but I doubt there will be a change for the better in the short-term future, at least not until investigations into the alleged meddling by Russia are completed. In my view, one development that could make the U.S. and Russia ignore the existing constraints

---

[33]"Putin otsenil chislennost' boyevikov iz byvshego SSSR v Sirii v 9 tysyach." RBC, February 23, 2017. Available at http://www.rbc.ru/politics/23/02/2017/58aee7b79a7947ee4af00978

[34] Richard Barrett. "Beyond the Caliphate: Foreign Fighters and the Threat of Returnees." Soufan Group, October 2017. Available at http://thesoufancenter.org/wp-content/uploads/2017/11/Beyond-the-Caliphate-Foreign-Fighters-and-the-Threat-of-Returnees-TSC-Report-October-2017-v3.pdf

[35] "Kremlin doubts report about 3,500 Russians fighting for Islamic State." TASS, October 26, 2017. Available at http://tass.com/politics/972644

[36] See for instance, Max Rosental. "Russia Has Killed Almost 10,000 Syrians in the Past Year, Says a New Report. That includes nearly 4,000 civilians," Mother Jones, September 20, 2016. Available at

and resume effective CT cooperation would be the one that we all would like to prevent the most—an act of nuclear terrorism. Should a terrorist-detonated mushroom cloud emerge anywhere in the world, it would become a game changer. In such a scenario I would imagine the U.S., Russia and their allies would jointly scramble together to prevent more attacks, as well as to find and punish not only the perpetrators but also the suppliers of the bomb and/or its components.

The author would like to thank Ted Siefer, assistant editor of the Russia Matters website, for assistance in research for this memo, and editor of the Russia Matters website Natasha Yefimova-Trilling for copyediting this statement.

Mr. POE. Dr. Carpenter, your opening statement.

STATEMENT OF MICHAEL CARPENTER, PH.D., NONRESIDENT SENIOR FELLOW, DINU PATRICIU EURASIA CENTER, ATLANTIC COUNCIL, SENIOR DIRECTOR OF THE BIDEN CENTER FOR DIPLOMACY AND GLOBAL ENGAGEMENT, UNIVERSITY OF PENNSYLVANIA

Mr. CARPENTER. Chairman Poe, Chairman Rohrabacher, Ranking Member Keating, and members of the committee, thank you for this opportunity to testify today.

President Putin and other Russian officials have long proposed that Russia and the United States should work more closely together on counterterrorism. President Trump has also said that we should work with Russia on CT. And at first glance it might seem natural that two nations that have suffered from terrorist attacks should collaborate more closely on fighting terrorism.

But this would be a grave mistake that damages our national security interests and runs contrary to our values. The Kremlin is, as has been said, a state sponsor of groups that use terrorist tactics against civilians. It is attacking the foundations of our democratic institutions and fueling conflicts from Syria to Afghanistan that contribute directly to radicalization and extremism.

In Ukraine, for example, the Kremlin directly contributed the missiles, the hardware, the training that resulted in the shooting down of Malaysia Airlines Flight 17, killing all 298 people on board. The Ukrainian intelligence services have also accused the Russian FSB of standing behind bombings of civilians in 2014 and 2015, as well as more recent vehicle-borne bomb attacks in the capital city of Kiev.

In Syria, the Kremlin's number one goal has been to prop up the murderous Assad regime, together with its allies, Lebanese Hezbollah and the Iranian Revolutionary Guards. Due to the involvement of its forces on the ground and in the air, Russia bears direct responsibility for the annihilation of the city of Aleppo, where civilian areas were indiscriminately bombed together with humanitarian relief convoys.

Let's not fool ourselves. Partnering with Russia in Syria would be the equivalent of partnering with Hezbollah or Iran. Indeed, Russia's military intervention in Syria has allowed its ally, Iran, to gain significant influence across the region, stretching from southern Iraq to southern Syria to Lebanon.

In Afghanistan, as has also been mentioned, Russia provides weapons to the Taliban, where these arms are likely used against U.S. CT forces and NATO-trained Afghan national forces. The Kremlin has taken this decision consciously, both to increase its influence in the region and to deliberately weaken the NATO Resolute Support mission.

Inside Russia itself, Russia's security forces are responsible for killings, torture, physical abuse, and politically motivated abductions. The Kremlin's strategy is not geared toward winning hearts and minds. Instead, its singular focus is on the physical liquidation of insurgents. Security forces in Russia, whether Federal or local, apply the principle of collective retribution against suspected militants. Russian CT operations also pay little regard for the possibility of civilian casualties among noncombatants.

Finally, Russian authorities have used the pretext of fighting extremism to crack down on Russia's democratic political opposition and other dissidents.

In the United States, Russia has tried to fan the flames of anti-Muslim xenophobia. Fake Russian accounts on Facebook and Twitter spread false allegations of crimes committed by Muslim migrants and try to stoke discord and hate in the very districts where your constituents live.

This has been happening for years. In 2015, the Russian-linked hacking group reportedly posed as an Islamic State front to mount a cyber attack on a French television network.

We should also remember that we have tried to partner with Russia on CT issues in the recent past. The results of these efforts indicate Russia is more interested in collecting intelligence on us than sharing information on terrorist threats.

Under a different Kremlin leadership it might make sense to work with Russia on CT operations or countering violent extremism. But today, the Putin regime's geopolitical ambitions and CT strategy are directly antithetical to U.S. national security, contribute directly to the radicalization of extremist groups, and are contrary to our basic values.

Thank you, and I look forward to answering your questions.

[The prepared statement of Mr. Carpenter follows:]

Testimony for the

Committee on Foreign Affairs
United States House of Representatives

Subcommittee on Terrorism, Nonproliferation, and Trade
and
Subcommittee on Europe, Eurasia, and Emerging Threats

November 7, 2017

"Russia: Counterterrorism Partner
or Fanning the Flames"

Dr. Michael Carpenter
Senior Director
Biden Center for Diplomacy and Global Engagement
University of Pennsylvania

Note: The statements, views, and policy recommendations expressed in this testimony reflect the opinions of the author alone, and do not necessarily reflect the positions of the Biden Center for Diplomacy and Global Engagement or the University of Pennsylvania.

Introduction

Chairman Poe, Chairman Rohrabacher, Ranking Member Keating, Ranking Member Meeks, and members of the Committee, thank you for this opportunity to speak with you today about Russia's strategy for fighting terrorism and the implications of trying to forge a closer U.S.-Russia counterterrorism (CT) partnership.

President Putin and other top Russian officials have long suggested that Russia and the United States should work more closely on counterterrorism. On 9/11, Putin was the first international leader to call President Bush to discuss the attack and offer Russia's support for closer counterterrorism cooperation. More recently, following its September 2015 military intervention in Syria, the Kremlin proposed that the United States and Russia cooperate militarily to fight the so-called Islamic State, currently one of the chief instigators of terrorism around the world.

At first glance, it might seem natural that two nations that have suffered from numerous terrorist attacks should collaborate more closely in fighting terrorism. Some argue that closer collaboration on counterterrorism could also improve our bilateral relationship as a whole and lead Moscow to adopt a more cooperative approach on other issues, thereby advancing U.S. national security interests.

Unfortunately, nothing could be further from the truth. The Kremlin is a state sponsor and ally of groups that use terrorist tactics against civilians, such as its separatist proxies in eastern Ukraine or the Shia militias with whom it cooperates in western Syria. Russia is also actively engaged in a covert struggle to undermine democratic institutions in the United States and among our Western allies. Under a different Kremlin leadership, therefore, it might make sense to work together on CT operations or countering violent extremism. But today, the Putin regime's geopolitical ambitions and CT strategy are antithetical to U.S. national security interests, contribute directly to the radicalization of extremist groups, and are contrary to our basic values.

Lest we forget, it is the current Russian regime that provided the missiles, the launcher, the software, the training, and perhaps even the triggerman to shoot down Malaysia Airlines Flight 17, killing all 298 people onboard. The Putin regime also deployed its military to Syria to annihilate Aleppo by indiscriminately bombing civilian areas and humanitarian convoys and reducing to rubble a city with a prewar population of 2.5 million people. And it is the Putin regime whose security forces are responsible for killings, torture, physical abuse, and politically motivated abductions across the Russian Federation. For these reasons, we should stay as far away from a CT partnership with Russia's current leadership as possible.

The Kremlin's Counterterrorism Strategy

Russia's counterterrorism strategy relies on overwhelming force to eliminate extremists. This strategy is not geared towards winning hearts and minds; its singular focus is physical liquidation of insurgents. During the Chechen wars of the 1990s, Russian federal authorities applied a scorched earth campaign that laid waste to entire villages that were perceived as fostering the insurgency. Russian military forces were notorious for carrying out human rights abuses such as abductions, summary executions, and torture. Both then and now, security forces in the North Caucasus republics of Chechnya, Dagestan, Ingushetia, North Ossetia, and Kabardino-Balkaria have applied the principle of collective retribution, often imprisoning, threatening, and sometimes even killing relatives of suspected militants. While some have described these tactics as brutal but effective, it has become clear that they are not just morally reprehensible but contribute to long-term radicalization of local communities. Such collective repression directly gives rise to the phenomenon of suicide bombings by "black widows" or other family members of slain or tortured insurgents who seek to avenge their kin.

Furthermore, Russian-led CT operations pay little regard to "collateral" civilian casualties among non-combatants. Russian security services' storming of the Dubrovka theater in Moscow in 2002 and their bungled attempt to free children and parents who were held hostage in a primary school in Beslan, North Ossetia in 2004 are both tragic examples of CT missions carried out with little regard for civilians, as evidenced by the more than 130 civilian casualties in Moscow and at least 385 (and possibly more) civilians killed in Beslan.

Equally disturbingly, Russian authorities have used the pretext of "fighting extremism" to crack down on Russia's democratic political opposition and other dissidents. Extremism is so broadly defined under Russia's current legal regime that it is has been used to imprison an investigative journalist for exposing official embezzlement, and sentence a 46-year-old single mother for posting information on social media that was critical of Russia's annexation of Crimea. The so-called Yarovaya law, named after Russian legislator Irina Yarovaya and enacted in July 2016, also amended Russian CT legislation to legalize mass surveillance by requiring telecommunications companies to retain all telephone and internet data for six months beginning in July 2018. Furthermore, the law bans preaching or praying outside of designated religious institutions and criminalizes the involvement of others in "mass unrest," a euphemism for organizing political protests.

Past Efforts at Counterterrorism Cooperation

The United States has tried many times in the past to cooperate with Russia on counterterrorism, and we should look closely at these efforts when evaluating the potential for future CT cooperation.

During the first term of the Obama administration, the U.S. and Russia established a Bilateral Presidential Commission that included a CT Working Group (among many others). At the direction of Presidents Obama and Medvedev, the group developed an ambitious agenda that included law enforcement cooperation, transportation security, intelligence sharing, terrorism finance, collaboration on counterterrorism technology, and coordination of U.S. and Russian positions within multilateral CT-oriented fora. Unfortunately, however, the working group proved to be a huge disappointment.

From 2010 - 2013, I served as the Deputy Director of the State Department's Office of Russian Affairs, where my role included overseeing the Commission's working groups. Although the co-chairs of the CT Working Group did meet a number of times during this period, the group failed to institutionalize any enduring law enforcement cooperation, intelligence sharing, or joint action on terrorism finance. From the start, it was clear that the Russian side was unwilling to discuss sensitive information and reluctant to speak about its own security vulnerabilities, which meant that working group sessions often devolved into an exchange of pleasantries and recitation of canned talking points. Joint events were held largely for show, such as a visit by Russian officials to Washington in May 2010 to learn about security measures on the U.S. rail system. As the U.S. coordinator of the CT Working Group, Daniel Benjamin, noted in an op-ed written earlier this year, "Russia's sclerotic bureaucracy and general lack of interest (especially with issues like deradicalization) made progress [on CT] impossible."

The terrorist bombing at Moscow's Domodedovo airport in January 2011 did spur bilateral discussions that resulted in a May 2011 Memorandum of Understanding between the U.S. Transportation Security Administration and Russia's Ministry of Transportation on security of civil aviation. In May 2011, the United States also formally designated the Caucasus Emirate – the primary terrorist group in Russia at the time – as a terrorist organization and included its leader, Doku Umarov, in the FBI's Rewards for Justice program. These moves were viewed positively by the Russian government. However, with Mr. Putin's return to the Kremlin in May 2012, bilateral relations began to deteriorate. In the fall of 2012, the Kremlin expelled the U.S. Agency for International Development (USAID) from Russia and informed the United States that it would be abrogating an agreement on law enforcement cooperation beginning in January 2013. This effectively put a stop to any real CT cooperation.

The exchange of information relating to the April 2013 Boston marathon bombing is often cited as an example of close CT cooperation during this period. Russia did indeed provide information to the FBI and CIA in 2011 informing the United States that suspected bomber Tamerlan Tsarnaev and his mother held extremist views, but the information was general and lacked any incriminating specifics. When the FBI's Legal Attaché in Moscow followed up in August 2011 with a written request for further information, the Russian government did not respond. After the bombing, however, Russia did grant access to U.S. law enforcement authorities to conduct interviews and gather additional information.

In mid-2013, U.S.-Russian relations deteriorated further as a result of Russia's decision to harbor former NSA contractor Edward Snowden. In spite of the Kremlin's increasingly adversarial approach during this period, however, the Sochi Olympics in February 2014 were simply too important for the United States not to make every effort to work collaboratively with Moscow to ensure the safety of the Games. In the fall of 2012, I traveled to Sochi at the invitation of the Russian government with a group of diplomatic, security, and intelligence officials from a select group of other countries to review Russia's security arrangements for the Games. We learned upon arriving in Sochi, however, that the senior Russian official who would be our chief interlocutor was not a CT expert, but rather the top counter-intelligence official in Russia's Federal Security Service (FSB). This was a telling indication of the Kremlin's primary focus as it prepared to host the Games. The following year, as an NSC Director for Russia, I also met bilaterally with counterparts from the Russian Security Council to discuss how we could expand information sharing on potential threats to the Olympics. Although the tone of these conversations was always cordial, the practical results were meager.

This is because Russia's strategy for protecting the Olympic Games from a terrorist attack rested on three basic pillars, none of which required cooperation with foreign partners. These included: (1) building an impenetrable security perimeter around the Olympic facilities and flooding the Olympic zone with Russian security agents; (2) employing massive force against insurgent communities in the neighboring North Caucasus federal republics; and (3) facilitating the movement of extremists from Russia to Syria. Particularly after the December 2013 Volgograd suicide bombing, which killed 32 civilians only months before the Opening Ceremonies, these efforts were accelerated. Although the Olympic Games themselves thankfully occurred without incident, Moscow's encouragement of insurgent travel to Syria will no doubt have lasting negative repercussions once the Islamic State collapses in Iraq and Syria and some of these fighters begin to return home.

Russia's Intervention in Syria: Fueling the Conflict

According to President Putin, the goal of Russia's intervention in Syria was to fight the Islamic State. This rationale has been belied, however, by Russia's airstrikes, which have overwhelmingly targeted the country's opposition to President Asad rather than the Islamic State. Some estimates put the ratio of airstrikes against the opposition versus the Islamic State at 4-to-1.

Russia has also prioritized constraining U.S. forces in the region over its fight against the Islamic State. For example, Moscow deployed sophisticated air defense systems to Syria such as the S-400 surface-to-air missile system, which is located at the Hmeymim airbase, and its most capable air-to-air fighters like the Su-30 and Su-35, despite the fact that neither the Islamic State nor any other extremist group in the region has access to air power. Clearly, these assets are meant to keep aircraft from the United States and other members of the counter-ISIS Coalition away Asad regime forces in western, central, and southern Syria.

Contrary to Putin's assertions, Russia's chief goal in Syria is to prop up the Asad regime. In addition to Syrian regime forces, its allies on the ground include Lebanese Hezbollah and the Iranian Revolutionary Guards, or Quds Force. Partnering with Russia to fight the Islamic State in Syria would therefore be tantamount to partnering with Hezbollah or Iran. This dynamic has only gotten worse as Iran has expanded its influence in the region. The agreement between President Trump and President Putin announced at the G20 summit in Hamburg to create "safe zones" in southern Syria has predictably created a backdoor for Russia's ally Iran to expand a so-called "Shia crescent" of influence stretching from southern Iraq and southern Syria into Lebanon. Russia's stoking of sectarian tensions between the Asad regime, Hezbollah, and Quds Force on the one hand and Sunni Arab groups on other, fuels the Syrian conflict and further radicalizes local Sunni communities.

Russia's fanning the flames of the Syrian conflict is made worse by its attacks on Syrian civilians. Russia's indiscriminate airstrikes using unguided "dumb bombs" and its blatant disregard for civilian casualties have radicalized many previous non-combatants. Moscow either fails to understand the consequences of its actions or chooses not to care. As a Deputy Assistant Secretary of Defense, I participated as part of an interagency delegation in negotiations with senior Russian military officers in August 2016 to try to find a way to deliver humanitarian aid to the then-besieged city of Aleppo. It was clear to me during these negotiations that the

Russian generals were playing for time as their forces closed in on Aleppo and that Moscow had no intention of allowing humanitarian assistance to reach civilian areas. Nevertheless, we tried in good faith to reach an agreement. Our Russian counterparts insisted disingenuously that Aleppo's civilian areas had been infiltrated by extremist Sunni groups and that humanitarian relief could be used to support these extremists. After devising a careful plan to ensure that only UN-monitored supplies would be let into these areas, the Russian military finally agreed. The following day, however, when Foreign Minister Lavrov flew to Geneva to meet with Secretary Kerry, he reneged on the agreement.

Today, Russia and the Asad regime have nearly complete control over central and western Syria, save for the Idlib region, which remains squarely within their sites. Less fortunately for the Kremlin, however, the fall of the Islamic State stronghold of Raqqa will likely precipitate the return of some of the roughly 2,500 Russian citizen fighters who joined the Syrian conflict.

Russia's Support for the Taliban in Afghanistan

In Afghanistan, Russia's provision of arms to the Taliban further testifies to its destabilizing role in the broader Middle East and Central Asia. Moscow's decision to support the Taliban aims to achieve four basic goals. First, the Kremlin is hedging its bets in case the Taliban comes back to power and breaks the current military stalemate with the Afghan government. Second, Moscow seeks to weaken the U.S.-led coalition and undermine the NATO-trained and equipped Afghan forces to accelerate the decline of U.S. power in the region. Third, by arming the Taliban, Moscow gains leverage and demonstrates it is a major regional actor that other powers like India and Pakistan must contend with. Finally, Moscow has an interest in empowering the Taliban to fight jihadist groups that Russia opposes, like the Islamic Movement of Uzbekistan (IMU), which has long been a thorn in Russia's side. Unfortunately, Moscow's support for the Taliban only fuels conflict and destabilizes the region over the long run.

Russia as a Malign International Actor

In addition to its destabilizing activities in Syria and Afghanistan, which have directly undermined U.S. interests, we must also not lose sight of the fact that Russia has trampled international law by inciting violence and deploying its forces to eastern Ukraine. Russia's activities in Afghanistan and Syria have fueled violent jihadism in the region, but in Ukraine, Russia itself has carried out targeted assassinations, sabotage, and operations that are frankly difficult to distinguish from state-sponsored terrorism. Ukraine's security services have blamed the recent spate of vehicle-born explosions in Kyiv squarely on Russia. In an unprecedented TV appearance this September, the head of the Security Service of Ukraine (SBU), Vasil Hrytsak, accused his Russian counterpart Aleksander Bortnikov, the head of the FSB, of not only standing behind prior bombings of civilians in Odessa, Kharkiv, and Kherson, but also of "breaking all rules" by planning to bomb Russian citizens in a series of false-flag operations intended to serve as a pretext for further violence against Ukraine.

Russia's Information War on the West

If Russia's activities elsewhere in the world were not enough to give one pause, we must ask ourselves what sort of CT partner Russia would make given its ongoing information war against the United States and our European partners and allies. In our own country, the Kremlin has sought to inflame racial tensions, deepen social divides, and set Americans against each other by spreading inflammatory rhetoric and lies. Russia has taken a particular interest in spreading propaganda on the topic of Muslim migrants, both in the United State and in Europe. Russian officials, for example, propagated the fake story that a Russian-German girl was raped by Muslim immigrants in Germany to stoke discord and set the public against German Chancellor Angela Merkel. In the United States, Russia trolls and social media accounts have also tried to fan the flames of anti-Muslim xenophobia. For example, the "Heart of Texas" Facebook account tried to stoke anti-Muslim feelings in Texas, while in Idaho the "SecuredBorders" site spread false allegations of rape that were used to incite anti-Muslim sentiments. Both accounts were tied to Russian trolls. Western cybersecurity companies have also revealed that the "CyberCaliphate" hacking group, which was believed to have been run by the Islamic State – and which hacked into one of the largest French television networks, TV5 – was actually a false-flag operation run by Russia's intelligence services.

How to Engage Russia on CT

Given Russia's actions around the world directly promoting and contributing to the spread of terrorism, should we then avoid all discussions of counterterrorism with Moscow? I believe there is a role for limited but persistent dialogue with Russia on CT issues, as long as we remain clear-eyed about Russia's aims and intentions.

First, given the proximity of Russian and Counter-ISIS Coalition forces in Syria, there is clearly a rationale for continuing the communications channel the Pentagon established with the Russian Ministry of Defense to deconflict operations in the air and on the ground. Both sides have an interest in avoiding an unintended escalation of the conflict, and despite Russia's clear pattern of trying to box the U.S. out of regions in Syria that it considers strategically important, this channel has nevertheless served a useful purpose.

Second, the United States must continue to share information with Russia through intelligence and law enforcement channels about plots against Russian officials and civilians. This is not only the moral and right thing to do, but it also demonstrates to Russia's security services that despite all their propaganda, the United States is willing to help protect Russian citizens.

Finally, though the chances of meaningful cooperation are slim, the United States should keep making extradition requests and using law enforcement channels to request information from Russia whenever there is a need. My experience of working with Russian officials shows that even if the Kremlin's grand strategy is to weaken the United States, there are officials within Russia's bureaucracy who genuinely want to cooperate or be helpful, and the more ties we cultivate with such officials, whether productive or not, the more channels of communication we have available in the event of a crisis.

Conclusion

Chairman Poe, Chairman Rohrabacher, Ranking Member Keating, Ranking Member Meeks, and members of the Committee, the United States government has no higher purpose than keeping its citizens safe and secure. That is why our CT policy has to be smart and leverage as many instruments of national power, hard and soft, as possible. In an ideal world, we would partner with Russia to keep our nations safe from the threat of terrorism and cooperate on issues like countering violent extremism or terrorism finance. However, the current Russian regime is misusing CT policy to suppress dissent, weaken the United States and NATO, and project Russia's global influence, often at our expense. Through the repression of its own citizens and alliances with hostile powers that foment terrorism, Moscow is fanning the flames of terrorism around the world. We should continue to communicate with Russia because we have no other choice, but we must do so with our eyes wide open, fully cognizant of the threat Moscow poses to our own security.

———————

Mr. POE. Thank you, Dr. Carpenter. And we understand that you have to leave at some time after 3 o'clock. Go ahead and excuse yourself. No one will arrest you on your way out the door.

Mr. CARPENTER. Chairman, I have to leave at 3:25.

Mr. POE. Alright, 3:25. We will watch the clock.

I will recognize myself for some questions, and then we will have the other members.

As you can see, there is a wide range of views among our two subcommittees on this issue. I want to talk specifically about the question at hand, Russia's involvement in terrorist activities. I would like to compare, if possible, Iran, which is labeled a state sponsor of terror—the number one state sponsor of terrorism in the world is Iran—with some of the actions of the Russians.

Dr. Carpenter, you mentioned the Malaysian plane that was shot down. Did the Russians shoot that down?

Mr. CARPENTER. Chairman, the Russians provided the system, the hardware, the missiles to infiltrate that system from Russia into Ukraine. We do not know who the triggerman was, but in all likelihood that person was trained in Russia by Russian special forces.

Mr. POE. Alright.

Does Russia, Dr. Cornell, supply arms and assistance to Hezbollah, a terrorist organization?

Mr. CORNELL. Sir, I don't have any more information on that than what I read in the papers. I read that that is the case. I don't have anything additional—I would call Russia the number one state manipulator of terrorism, if that is helpful.

Mr. POE. That is a new term that we may have to deal with.

Do any of the other three of you wish to comment on whether Russia does or does not supply any materials to Hezbollah, a terrorist group?

Dr. Carpenter.

Mr. CARPENTER. So, Chairman, I can't speak directly to whether they contribute weapons or material. However, it is clear that Russian special forces on the ground in Syria coordinate their actions with their allies, their principal allies being Assad regime forces, Hezbollah forces, and the Quds Force from Iran.

Mr. POE. So they work with them. They may not supply material support, but they work on the same side, so to speak, in supporting the Assad regime.

Mr. CARPENTER. Sir, they coordinate both tactical and strategic missions.

Mr. POE. Is the elimination of journalists, political opponents—I alluded to 14 of them in my opening statement that were suddenly disappeared by so-called accidents in the United Kingdom—was that inspired or supported or done by the Russian Government? Do any of you want to comment on that?

Dr. Carpenter again.

Mr. CARPENTER. So, Chairman, we know that the U.K. Government has fingered two Russians, Andrei Lugovoi and his partner, in the murder of Alexander Litvinenko with polonium, and they have provided a great deal of information about how that was done specifically. And I think I will leave it at that.

Mr. POE. Would any of you consider cyber attacks by one nation, specifically Russia, into the United States, would you consider that terrorism, an act of war, or something else?

Dr. Cornell.

Mr. CORNELL. Mr. Chairman, I think, depending on what that cyber attack does, it could be any of the above.

I think the important part to understand about Russia is that the advantage they have, in spite of the weakness in terms of economic power and the vulnerability of their political system, is that they have a highly hierarchical power vertical, as Mr. Putin likes to call it, that has a whole different set of instruments, a toolbox, that they can choose from. They can use direct military attacks on their neighbors, as in the cases of Ukraine and Georgia. They can choose to use cyber attacks, subversion, support or manipulation of insurgency.

All of these are available to Mr. Putin through the press of a button. We are not organized to respond to that type of behavior from a state like Russia, and I think that is really where the problem is.

Mr. POE. Any of the rest of you want to comment on that?

Dr. Clarke.

Mr. CLARKE. Not specifically on cyber, but to get back to one of your earlier points about the Russians and Lebanese Hezbollah. I think if Iran is a state sponsor of terrorism, Russia is a sponsor of a state sponsor of terrorism by sponsoring the Iranian regime and working closely to deconflict with Lebanese Hezbollah on the ground.

Mr. POE. State sponsor of a sponsor of terrorism. Alright. Okay.

Let me ask you one other question, the four of you, just yes or no. Should the United States work with Russia in trying to combat international terrorism?

Dr. Clarke.

Mr. CLARKE. No.

Mr. POE. Dr. Cornell.

Mr. CORNELL. Not under the current regime in Russia, sir.

Mr. POE. Not under Putin.

Dr. Saradzhyan.

Mr. SARADZHYAN. In my view, if there is a credible, serious threat to the United States posed by terrorist groups, then the answer should be yes.

Mr. POE. Dr. Carpenter.

Mr. CARPENTER. We should not cooperate with Russia. We should communicate with them, but under no circumstances should we cooperate.

Mr. POE. Okay. Thank you.

The Chair will recognize the gentleman from Massachusetts.

Mr. KEATING. Thank you, Mr. Chairman.

Since Dr. Carpenter is leaving, I am intrigued on one thing. I traveled to Sochi prior to the beginning of the Winter Olympics to learn more. It was a two-person codel. Frankly, we had some difficulty getting in, but we made it in there. And both Members of Congress were very surprised when we got there.

We were there to look at the cooperation that exists and how we could learn from that with a major event. When we got there it was clear that there was cooperation with almost every other country working together and with our FBI and other intelligence people that were there, but it was a total wall with Russia, which I found odd because that is their sovereign area and we have a vested interest, I think, in pooling those resources.

So, Dr. Carpenter, you gave me maybe an answer as to at least why that was the case. I thought it was just one of sovereignty and pride, but you have a different theory in part. So I am very intrigued. Could you expound on that?

Mr. CARPENTER. So, Ranking Member Keating, I also traveled to Sochi as part of an international set of security, diplomatic, and intelligence officials to discuss preparations for security arrangements in advance of the games. It was clear then that the Russians were not willing to divulge a great deal of information about the preparations that were underway, other than that they were creating a massive perimeter around the Olympic facilities, and they intended to——

Mr. KEATING. The ring of steel, right?

Mr. CARPENTER. The ring of steel, as it was called, correct, sir.

But at the time our chief interlocutor on the Russian side was the top FSB general responsible for counterintelligence, not counterterrorism, Mr. Syromolotov, and it was clear from the engagements that we had at the time that their primary concern was counterintelligence and not sharing information on terrorist threats.

Later, subsequently, when I was NSC director for Russia, we engaged in bilateral conversations with the Russian Security Council on Sochi, which I participated in, and I have to say the tone of those conversations was very cordial. The mood was okay. But we did not receive any significant information from the Russians in the leadup to the games, despite having an enormous interest in terms of being the largest sponsor with the largest number of athletes and the largest number of sportsmen contributing to the games.

Mr. KEATING. Thank you.

I think it was Dr. Cornell. If it wasn't, I will let anyone jump in. But I was intrigued because you can look at it from the other side and say, you know, why wouldn't it be in Russia's interest to cooperate with us?

And I think it was Dr. Cornell who said in your opening remarks that they are doing it because they have a unique regime and they want to protect that regime. If it wasn't Dr. Cornell, please anyone who wants to answer this.

But what did you mean by preservation of their unique regime and why this is the way they conduct themselves in terms of counterterrorism and other actions to preserve that uniqueness?

Mr. CORNELL. Ranking Member Keating, what I referred to was specifically and primarily Russia's behavior toward its neighbors. It was very much predicated on an answering to the so-called color revolutions in Georgia, Ukraine, and Kurdistan from 2003 to 2005, which the Russian Government saw as a mortal threat to its own form of government.

Because if those neighboring states would be able to develop into successful democracies, especially if Ukraine, which shares linguistic and cultural ties with Russia, if Ukrainians would be able to live in a state that was not authoritarian, not corrupt, not kleptocratic—why should the Russian population itself tolerate continuing to live under those circumstances.

And therefore what had previously been mainly a geopolitical, board game type Realpolitik relationship with the West became very ideological. For Russia after that, undermining the very notion of democracy, popular support for democracy, both among its neighbors, among the Russian public itself, and even in the West, became an aim of the regime, because by discrediting democracy, and especially democratic uprisings and revolutions, and making the West appear to be chaotic and decadent, that bolstered support domestically for the Russian regime itself. That is mainly when I referred to.

But part of that is also undermining the leadership of the United States in the world, including—and that is one of the main reasons why Russia moved to Syria, not because—partly because Syria is important to Russia, but also because they saw a vacuum that enabled them——

Mr. KEATING. If I could interrupt for 2 seconds, I just have one more question. Because I think it is maybe more than ideological. How much is Putin worth? How much would you estimate, any of you?

Mr. CORNELL. I have heard figures of $40 billion, but that was a long time ago.

Mr. KEATING. Anyone else want to venture a guess?

Mr. CARPENTER. So, Ranking Member Keating, I can't hazard a guess because Putin is the beneficial owner through a variety of shell corporations and accounts. Other people hold money for him. But it is in the billions of dollars, likely the tens of billions of dollars.

Mr. KEATING. I would just suggest that maybe it is a little bit more than ideological.

And I yield back.

Mr. POE. I thank the gentleman.

The Chair recognizes the gentleman from Florida, Mr. Mast.

Mr. MAST. Thank you, Chairman.

And thank you, gentlemen, for your testimony.

I am of the mind that I don't believe that Russian intervention in Syria was by any means a counterterrorism objective. I think it was certainly a counterinsurgency objective against those that would have stood against Assad.

I think in doing that you could say that they stepped in it. I think that would be a good way to put it. I think the terrorist activities that have resulted in Russia are proof of that. There have been calls for jihad, obviously by ISIS, by al-Nusrah. There are estimates of 5,000 to 7,000 Russians that are over there fighting on behalf of the Islamic State.

And that brings me to my first question. Do you think that Russia is going to allow those thousands of fighters back into Russia? What is your speculation or take on that piece of it?

By all means, sir.

Mr. CLARKE. Absolutely not. I mean, I think that was part and parcel of the strategy in the leadup to Syria, was to usher these individuals out and to encourage them to go to Syria, full well knowing that the Russian Air Force would then bomb them from the skies and then put up a fairly robust border security forest to prevent anyone from returning home, although that does not prevent the radicalization of individuals who were prevented from leaving, never left in the first place.

Mr. MAST. That kind of creates a very good segue for my followup question. It has been said within Russian counterterrorism efforts that the family is the thread that needs to be pulled to unravel a terror group.

Could any of you unpack that a little bit in terms of whether that has been a successful policy within the borders of Russia for Vladimir Putin?

Mr. CARPENTER. So I can start, I think Dr. Clarke has also written and spoken about this.

But collective retribution is one of the policies that especially local security forces use in Chechnya, Ingushetia, Dagestan, and the other North Caucasus Federal Republics. It is singularly ineffective.

Some analysts will tell you that it is brutal but effective in the short run, but over the long run clearly it is myopic and leads to radicalization of entire communities who feel that the regime is bearing done upon them. But it is common for family members of insurgents or would-be militants to be kidnapped, to be tortured, to be interrogated, held, sometimes even killed.

Mr. MAST. Any further? Please, by all means.

Mr. SARADZHYAN. I would like to point out that according to Russia's independent Meduza newsline outlet, whose journalists have gone and interviewed people in the North Caucasus, Ingushetia has set up, one of the republics in the North Caucasus, has set up a commission to try to accommodate some of the people who tried to return from Syria to Russia.

But I would be very surprised if a large number of individuals would use that channel because they are still liable according to the Russian law and they would be jailed if tried and convicted for participation in illegal formations.

There has also been an effort to bring in wives and children of the killed rebels, and that has been done in the North Caucasus, and I think the numbers is in dozens.

But again, 5,000 people fighting and only dozens of cases being successfully returned to Russia.

Thank you.

Mr. CLARKE. Sir, I can speak to some of the empirical evidence that I have come across in my own research on this topic. I was one of the coauthors at RAND of a study on counterinsurgency looking at every single insurgency since the end of World War II to 2009. We roundly found that what we call the "crush them" approach, a draconian, authoritarian approach to counterinsurgency, was indeed counterproductive in the long term.

Mr. MAST. Very good.

I have one more question and this is open to any one of you. All of you said pretty much unanimously that we should not cooperate with Russia. That is a very ambiguous statement when we are talking about counterterrorism.

So please, if any of you could give me some examples of normal counterterrorism cooperation that would exist between nations that you believe we should not undertake. Give me some concrete examples of what you wouldn't like to see happen in terms of counterterrorism cooperation, that being the word that you all used.

Mr. CARPENTER. Perhaps I can start again and I will have to leave after this.

But in terms of counterterrorism cooperation, I would not want the U.S. Government to be sharing any information that could compromise sources or methods. I would not want the U.S. Government to share any information with the Russian Government that could be used against dissidents inside Russia.

And certainly, I would not want the U.S. military to be engaging in any sort of combat missions or operations or sharing of information on targets in Syria or any other military battlefield, because that would essentially make the U.S. complicit in any civilian casualties that result from Russia's bombing campaign, as well as it would tie us to the toxic axis that Russia has formed with Hezbollah and Iran that we have spoken about earlier.

Mr. MAST. My time has expired. If the chairman wishes to give you all time to answer, by all means, but I thank you for your responses.

Mr. POE. I thank the gentleman from Florida.

The Chair recognizes the gentleman from New York, Mr. Meeks.

Mr. MEEKS. Thank you, Mr. Chairman.

I know you have got to go, Dr. Carpenter, and I was going to ask a very similar question as Mr. Mast, and I guess you just answered it. Because I wanted to know specifically what U.S. interests that cooperation would undermine. And I think basically you just said that there are several intelligence pieces that Mr. Putin. So just in case, is there anything that you wanted to add to that before you leave?

Mr. CARPENTER. Well, I think the only other thing I would say is that we all have to remember that Russia right now is engaged in an ongoing attack against our democratic institutions.

Russia sees the United States as its chief geopolitical adversary for some of the reasons that my friend Svante has outlined, namely that it sees the United States and the West, Western democracies, as the ones who are undermining its kleptocratic and authoritarian regime. So, to protect its wealth and power it is striking out against the United States and other countries.

And for us to be engaged in a cooperative effort at the very same time that Russia is attacking our institutions and seeking to gain advantage over the United States and our military just doesn't make sense to me.

Mr. MEEKS. You have answered. I am going to ask this to all of the panelists.

I think President Trump has recently suggested that cooperation with Russia on counterterrorism efforts should lead to sanctions relief on Ukraine. Now, I have my own opinion, but let me just ask you for your opinion. Should that lead to sanctions relief? Should a counterterrorism agreement with Russia lead to sanctions relief with Ukraine?

Mr. CLARKE. I am sure Moscow would love that and that would be the intended purpose of any kind of proposed cooperation. But I think as you said, Ranking Member Meeks, in your own opening statement, Russian self-interest will occasionally intersect with ours and it is nothing more beyond that.

Mr. CORNELL. If I may add, Ranking Member Meeks, I think this is exactly the mistake that the Obama administration did after Russia invaded Georgia following years of using insurgents to undermine the sovereignty of that country.

As you know, only months after that any sanctions that had been imposed on Russia by the U.S. and Europe were tabled and the reset policy was started which sent a signal to Russia that: We can do whatever we want to, the West will back off, and will cooperate with us again.

And I think that is exactly the signal that we would send by doing, and by doing so, we would set ourselves up for even larger troubles with Russia in the future.

The only way to get Russia to be a constructive partner is to show them what is acceptable behavior and what it not. Once they have understood that, I am all for cooperation.

Mr. MEEKS. Dr. Carpenter.

Mr. CARPENTER. I generally agree with that statement. As someone who was working on Georgia policy at the time though, I would simply add that the Obama administration took office in late January and the Bush administration made absolutely no effort to put sanctions on Russia for its invasion of Georgia, nor impose any other lasting consequences, which was a mistake.

Mr. MEEKS. Thank you.

Let me go back. Dr. Cornell, real quick. I think, if I am not mistaken, you were a witness at a hearing that we had on Azerbaijan a few years ago. And you recently wrote about how the United States inadvertently promotes extremism, right, in the name of religious freedom, if I am not correct.

Mr. CORNELL. Yes, sir.

Mr. MEEKS. Which goes to show how blanket policies can be dangerous in the local politics.

What missed opportunities are there in Central Asia for cooperation with Russia, in your opinion?

Mr. CORNELL. Ranking Member Meeks, I think there are enormous opportunities for cooperation in Central Asia with the governments and states of Central Asia. They would like to cooperate with us directly. They don't need any intermediaries.

With Russia, we know that one of the reasons why Russia in 2010 supported the ouster of the government of Kyrgyzstan was because that government refused to eject the United States military base that was existing in that country. That triggered the move by Russia against that government, led to a coup d'etat, which was followed by large-scale ethnic unrest in the south of that country. So, subsequently, the U.S. military base in Kurdistan was closed.

I think that tells you everything you need to know about how Russia would view any form of cooperation with the United States in Central Asia.

However, as I said, these are countries that are attempting, in spite of many domestic flaws in terms of human rights, freedoms, and so on, to build secular states in the Muslim world. We have not acknowledged that. That was the subject of the article that you referred to that I cowrote with two colleagues. We have tended to hector them about not respecting religious freedom without understanding that they are trying to maintain secular societies, secular systems of education and law. And that is something where we can cooperate with them.

Mr. MEEKS. Thank you.

I think I am out of time, so I will yield back.

Mr. POE. The Chair recognizes Chairman Rohrabacher for his questions.

Mr. ROHRABACHER. Thank you very much, Mr. Chairman. There is a lot of ground to cover and I am the only over here trying to present an alternative right now.

But let me just note that after 9/11 I think that we could say that there is no other country in the world that did more to help cooperate and had a major influence on what we did to defeat the Taliban and kick Saddam Hussein out. They made their bases available to us, because we came in from the north, instead of through Pakistan.

And the reason we didn't go through Pakistan, because Pakistan and Saudi Arabia were the ones who invented the Taliban, who we were at that point going to war with because they had slaughtered 3,000 Americans, their Taliban. And also the Saudis, who almost all of the hijackers were Saudis. Okay? But Russia stepped up. That doesn't count, does it? No, we are good friends with the Saudis and the Paks.

Let me just get in a couple of things. I am sorry the gentleman had to leave. I don't know if he—it sounded like he was or was not suggesting that the Russians were culpable in the shooting down of that aircraft.

But let's just note that we support a lot of groups all over the world. Do we have a double standard here? Is that what it is all about, if the Russians can do something, but that doesn't apply to the United States when we support people and they do some bad things with the weapons that we give them?

I think that if I was a Russian listening to this, that is what I would come to the conclusion of: Oh, the Americans have this double standard.

I am going to ask one question, I am sorry again, very quickly. Can any of you tell me why the Russians gave $150 million to the Clinton Foundation when Hillary Clinton was the Secretary of State? Can anybody tell me on the witness stand?

Okay. Well, that shouldn't be out of the equation. When we are trying to discuss what Russia does, we know that that happened, even though there seems to be an effort to try to cover that up and now don't pay attention to it.

Assad. Is Assad demonstrably different than any number of five or six other dictatorships in the Middle East? Is he capable more, if any of those people had uprisings in their country, is he capable, is he doing more than what they would do to destroy the uprising?

Mr. CLARKE. Chairman Rohrabacher, I would note that Assad has used chemical weapons twice against his own population, and that seems to be more than anyone else has done in the region.

Mr. ROHRABACHER. How many people were killed in that? So we are talking about——

Mr. CLARKE. How many——

Mr. ROHRABACHER. Yeah, using chemical weapons is bad. Using a rocket bomb that kills 10 times as many people is bad as well. And the bottom line is, I have heard this chemical, biological. Yes, I am against chemical biological weapons.

But what is important here is the number of people who are being—civilians especially—who are being killed to intimidate them. And the bottom line is Assad is a bad guy. So are a bunch of regimes that we support there.

And let us also suggest this, that Assad has had a chance to be a force for peace with Israel all of these decades, and that should be taken into consideration when we judge Assad.

And also let us note about Russian support for Assad, the Russians tried to convince us: Look, we can make a deal with Qadhafi, it will settle things down, it is better than what will happen if Qadhafi is overthrown.

The same thing with Saddam Hussein. Now they are trying to tell us that is true with Assad. What are the chances? Think about, what are the chances, Assad is overthrown, that you get a radical Islamic government that hates us and is willing to support terrorism? The chances are very high.

And when we discuss these things, those things should be in our calculation as to what our policies should be and they don't seem to be. What we seem to be talking about is everybody's—the faults of anybody who is associated with Russia. Let's note that we have some of those same faults and we shouldn't have a double standard.

And I noticed the last time, Mr. Chairman, that we had this whole bombing attack, I remember there was 84 civilians that were killed in that hospital and nobody would justify that.

But I would have to suggest that since we invaded and tried to get out of Saddam Hussein, and even right now in our efforts to try to overcome the radicals and Assad's forces, many, many thousands of people, civilians, have lost their lives to American bombs. Not intentionally that we wanted to single them out, but that that was the byproduct of that.

And I would just suggest that if we want to have peace in this world, especially with radical Islam the way it is, we better work and not have a double standard and try to work with people, as we needed to when we defeated Hitler. And otherwise Hitler would not have been destroyed, and Stalin was really was an awful person.

Thank you very much, Mr. Chairman.

Mr. POE. The Chair recognizes the gentleman from New Jersey.

Mr. SIRES. Thank you, Mr. Chairman. After those 5 minutes I have to collect my thoughts. They are kind of scrambled.

So, first of all, I would like to associate myself with the comments of the chairman and the ranking member. I certainly agree with you 100 percent.

I grew up in Cuba. I left in 1962. I think I know a little bit about Communism. And I remember very clearly when they started the indoctrination process, when they started trying to inculcate into your mind that the things in the world that are wrong were wrong because of the United States, that we were the evil of the world, that we needed to destroy the United States of America. Fortunately, I was taken out of that situation and brought to this country.

And I don't know anywhere in this world where the Russians have a footprint that is better off today than before. They create nothing but chaos, they create nothing but destruction, because that is how they thrive.

Because if you give those countries the ability to stop and think what Russia stands for—what that government stands for—and I am not saying the Russian people are bad, but that government, people will never accept that.

So, unfortunately, you know, this is such a great country that we have my colleague from California different from me, and he will go home and he will have coffee and everything else. He will have the Kool-Aid, too, regarding Russia.

But I just don't know anywhere in the world where they are better off when the Russians are in. I remember we came close to nuclear war when they tried to put nuclear weapons 90 miles away from here.

We had a visit, we had a defector here the other day from Korea, and he stated that the reason North Korea has developed such rapid nuclear weapons is because the Russians have helped them develop it.

Now, is that someone we can work with? I mean really, my thoughts are still scrambled.

So I really don't have any questions, Chairman, because I am kind of, you know, I am, like, flabbergasted that somebody can think of Russia and think so much of it. If I were in Russia, Dana, I would hire you. I would hire you as a lobbyist here in this country.

Mr. ROHRABACHER. You mean like they did with Hillary?

Mr. SIRES. That is right, Hillary and you.

Mr. WILSON. It was Bill that got the money.

Mr. SIRES. Look, as I look at this and I see what is going on now in the Western Hemisphere where the Russians are trying to influence and trying to damage any kind of a system that you have there, they are arming Nicaragua in the Western Hemisphere, they are propping up a regime in Venezuela that is the destruction of Venezuela. I mean, as you look, obviously, they just opened up the hearing in Cuba, they had a whole big hearing to eavesdrop on Americans' communication, it is all open now.

So, I just can't buy the fact that we can somehow work with this government. I would not trust any information that we get from Russia if we were ever working together. And when you talk about Putin, he is KGB years ago and he is KGB now.

And the KGB's mission was to destroy this country, and we saw what they did in this election. And we are still feeling the effects of this election where we have our groups at each other's throats because of what Russia did in this country by hacking all these different places.

So, Chairman, I thank you for holding this hearing. And I yield back the rest of my time.

Mr. WILSON [presiding]. Thank you, Congressman Sires. And we appreciate so much your Cuban American heritage and your strength on behalf of freedom in Cuba.

Chairman Poe has assigned myself for the balance of the hearing. He had an additional meeting that he would be attending.

At this time I will defer to myself for questions, Congressman Joe Wilson from South Carolina.

With the collapse of the Soviet Union, which was correctly identified by Ronald Reagan as the Evil Empire, I was so hopeful for a new modern Russia participating in Europe, participating in Asia, positively participating around the world.

And I have visited Russia a number of times. It is always very impressive to me, the wonderful people, the positive people who I met, the extraordinary Russian culture, the art, the music, the literature, the architecture.

But, sadly, with the Putin regime there has been a return to an authoritarian status, which I think is so disappointing for what should be such a positive country.

Russia has taken strong action against terrorism domestically, as it is a fertile field for radical Islamic terrorists, as we all, sadly, saw with the massacre at the school in Beslan.

Also, they have targeted ISIS and other groups that have infringed on them in their allies. But, sadly, in other cases they have supported Iranian-backed militia through their support of the Assad regime in Syria.

In any of your opinions, does Russia actually have a strong, coherent antiterrorism policy or do they have a policy of convenience? And by that, they seem to support destablizing efforts of terrorism when the action supports a short-term strategic goal of Russia and ignore the long-term effects of supporting terrorist organizations which one day would actually come back to kill Russian citizens.

And we can begin with Dr. Clarke or whoever would like to proceed.

Mr. CORNELL. I would like just to bring up one example, sir, which is a man by the name of Shamil Basayev. This was Russia's terrorist number one for a number of years until he died in 2006. This is a person that Russia trained to fight in the insurgency against Georgia and Abkhazia in 1991 to 1992.

After a few years, he came back and became the leader of the jihadi resistance in Chechnya, which shows an exact example of what you are talking about, namely, how Russia themselves created their owns Frankensteins, if you will, that came to hit back against Russia. That is because their policy is shortsighted and tactical in nature rather than long term and strategic.

Mr. WILSON. Dr. Clarke.

Mr. CLARKE. Thank you, Congressman.

I would add to that, as I have alluded to in my written testimony, that several prominent individuals from the former Soviet Union, including an individual known colloquially as Omar the Chechen, rose to fairly high ranks within the Islamic State. It kind of shows the prominence with which certain Russians have attained within ISIS.

And so, that would be one of my main concerns, you know, were I Russia, for kind of blowback in the aftermath of the collapse of the caliphate.

Mr. SARADZHYAN. I would like to point out that this particular individual, if you are referring to the minister of war, he was actually a native of Georgia, ethnic Chechen, he wasn't Russian national or ethic Russian.

In general, I would like to point out that terrorism is a strategy. I condemn that strategy because it targets innocent people, but whether a country actively pursues terrorists, unfortunately, it many times depends on what national interests are. Okay?

But if you look at the national interests of the U.S. and Russia, I would still argue that it is in the vital interest of both countries to prevent innocent people being killed by terrorists. So in that sense, whenever lives of innocent people are at state, I would suggest cooperation with Russia, with any other country for that matter, that can prevent killing of innocent people.

Thank you.

Mr. WILSON. Thank you each.

Russia's aggression into the Ukraine—and it should be remembered that 10,000 people have died due to that aggression—and support for pro-Russian separatists in Ukraine, of the Republic of Georgia—I just returned from Tbilisi. What an extraordinary country, and how brave the people are of the Republic of Georgia and what great allies they are of the United States. Also, there has been destabilization in Moldova.

And would you view their direct support for government separatists as supporting terrorism and another example of antiterrorist policy of convenience? In addition, should the United States consider these groups terrorist organizations? I would like your input on that.

Mr. CORNELL. So definitely in Ukraine we see examples of terrorist tactics being used. And the other conflicts we would have to go back to events in the early 1990s. We could discuss what was terrorism and what was not. But in Ukraine definitely.

Mr. WILSON. And my time is up. Part of being chairman, we have to abide by the time.

And so I would like now to proceed could Congresswoman Robin Kelly of Illinois.

Ms. KELLY. Thank you, Mr. Chairman.

As the United States works to defeat the Islamic State there are opportunities to work with Russia, but the U.S. must create clear lines when working together on counterterrorism. The Russian tactics of indiscriminate bombing and targeting of civilian populations run contrary to our values and the long-term benefits of counterterrorism. The Kremlin's support of nonstate actors that align with their interests also endangers any potential partnership in the Middle East as doing so legitimizes rogue actors and discourages long-term stability.

In addition to interfering in our elections with propaganda, the top U.S. general in Afghanistan, General John Nicholson, testified that Russia is trying to legitimize the Taliban by spreading a false narrative that the Taliban is fighting the Islamic State. These are very concerning developments that undermine our ability to build mutual trust between the U.S. and Russia.

So to the panel, given Russia's extremely poor track record on human rights, how should the U.S. cooperate with Russia without undermining our American values? In addition, what assurances should we seek from Russia? And what are the potential risks of increasing counterterror operations?

I can repeat it again if that is too long.

Mr. CLARKE. Thank you very much for your question, Congresswoman.

As I have stated, I don't think the United States should cooperate with Russia, I don't think that Russia is a reliable partner. I think that Russia is not accountable to its own citizens. And as you mentioned, the human rights abuses are one example of that.

And I think just the lack of trust that permeates the overall relationship speaks volumes. There is a reason for that lack of trust. And I haven't see seen any evidence or any reasons of why that lack of trust should have dissipated.

Ms. KELLY. Thank you.

Mr. CORNELL. Congresswoman, I concur with the previous speaker.

Ms. KELLY. The other panelist?

Mr. SARADZHYAN. As I have said before, I think whenever lives of innocent people are at stake, that countries should cooperate to prevent killing of innocent people.

And the domestic order in Russia—Russia is no democracy, of course. It is a semi-authoritarian regime, but what is the vital interest? Is that preventing terrorist attacks against citizens of a country? I think it is a vital interest. So acting with Russia in that interest would benefit the United States, in my view.

At the same time, of course, given the current atmosphere and the rivalry between the two countries, it is difficult to expect any kind of golden age we saw relatively robust cooperation when the Bilateral Commission was established.

So for Russia to be embraced as a full partner in this sphere, as I said, several things should happen. The conflict in Ukraine should be resolved, the conflict in Syria should be resolved, and these conflicts can be resolved, although the one in Ukraine is difficult to resolve.

But even if these things happen, we have to wait for results of the congressional and the FBI inquiries, because these would determine the scope of cooperation or rivalry or whatever happens between the United States and Russia in this sphere.

Thank you.

Ms. KELLY. It seems like the President has this expectation that Russia can help us with North Korea. Do you see that at all?

Mr. CORNELL. Congresswoman, as I noted in my opening remarks, I think the problem with Russia is that when confronted with a choice between either supporting the United States in solving an international problem, even one that may be problematic for Russia on the one hand, and taking a course of action that would further undermine the interests of the United States, Russia chooses the latter option. And that is why I think it is highly unlikely.

I think at this point Russia is probably, after China has shown tendencies of becoming fed up with North Korea, Russia—I wouldn't be surprised if they turned out to be the major lifeline of the North Korean regime in the years going forward.

Mr. CLARKE. Congresswoman, I think any cooperation with Russia needs to be viewed within the broader relation, and also within the broader set of Moscow's geopolitical ambitions, and not through the narrow lens, whether it is cooperation in Syria or the North Korea problem set. I think we need to look at this more comprehensively.

Mr. SARADZHYAN. I think Russia's participation in the talks with Iran on its nuclear program has showed that despite of certain deterioration of the relationship, when it is in the vital interest of Russia to attain a certain outcome, it can cooperate.

I see Russia's vital interest in having no nuclear neighbors. So if we want to continue down the diplomatic path, you could expect Russia to behave accordingly in the United Nations Security Council. But if the path of war had been chosen, Russia would probably oppose that path because it is located next to North Korea and it just doesn't want a major conflict on its borders.

That said, we should bear in mind that Russia's leverage vis—vis North Korea is fairly limited. And the only country that is considered as a lifeline for North Korea is China. If China stops supplies, North Korean Government will not last long. So it if there is a country where there is a silver bullet, so to say, the country is China, not Russia.

Ms. KELLY. Thank you. I yield back.

Mr. WILSON. Thank you very much, Congresswoman Kelly.

We now proceed to Congressman Scott Perry of Pennsylvania.

Mr. PERRY. Thanks, Mr. Chairman.

I find it fascinating, some of the dialogue today. Just my mind wanders from one point to another.

Sir, where you just said that Russia would oppose action in North Korea because it doesn't want conflict on its borders, yet I don't know, to anybody that is noticing world events on a daily basis, Russia creates conflict on every single border every single day, unprovoked, in my opinion.

But that having been said, like I said, I am curious about the meaning of this hearing or the reason for this hearing. I mean, Russia has been a strategic adversary, if not an outright enemy since its existence. And yet, we have people—and they confront America from without and within every single day. And it is well documented. It is well documented. And we have had Presidents cooperating, I mean, to the height of the Presidency.

Once again, I must mention Mr. Harry Hopkins. And how about John Service working within the FDR administration? The heck with working within the administration, working in the Oval Office with the President. I mean, the history is replete.

That having been said, I have just got to say that I think that we must separate the Russian people generally from the apparatchik, from the management, if you will, the leadership of the country. I think the people, generally speaking, of the Russia have a different mindset and would like to lead a different life to a certain extent, devoid of what the actions and the aims and interests of their leadership are. But there are two different things and we are dealing with their leadership.

And I also must say that any kind equivocation or moral equivalency by some Members of this august body up here at the dais that the United States in its interest is similar to Russians and their interests when we inadvertently hurt civilians in some kind of a campaign, where the Russians don't care about hurting civilians, that is a very stark difference and I think it is important to draw that.

That having been said, nations acting in their own self-interest—and Russia is going to act in its own self-interest and always has. And I would agree with Dr. Clarke and Dr. Cornell, particularly, I think, that would say that any time that they can use it against the United States in particular, even sometimes irrationally, that they seem to be willing to do that and they have a history of doing that.

But I have one curiosity at a minimum: The Tsarnaev brothers, the Boston Marathon bombing where allegedly they tipped off. I say "allegedly" because these days you just don't what the truth about anything is reported from anywhere.

But if they did inform our intelligence community in the United States in advance, what would have been their interest in doing that? I mean, were they just being Good Samaritans, I mean, at that level, or is there a different game here? Is it every now and then you throw the dog a bone and the big one is, "We are going to take over this country over here while you guys watch the Tsarnaev brothers blow up your marathon"? What is your opinion on that?

Mr. CLARKE. I can't speak to what Russian interests might have been in providing that information or whether, if that information was provided, if it was a complete picture. What I can say is whatever information was provided did not prevent an attack still.

And I would also say I agree with you that I think nations will always act in their own self-interest, but we should not mistake that with altruism.

Mr. CORNELL. Congressman, on the issue of the Tsarnaev brothers, I think I know little about this, the intelligence agencies know more, but it seems to me that intelligence agencies always trade with one another. And any information provided to the United States would be in the expectation of requiring something more valuable in return.

Mr. PERRY. Fair enough.

Alright. So you have Georgia, you have Ukraine, you have Syria, but it is a little bit of a different circumstance, in my opinion. We opened the door for Russia to go in, as opposed to Russia creating the opportunity.

With the diminishing time that I have, you have, like I said, Georgia and Ukraine in particular. I would say, who is next based on the model that Russia has used of creating the problem and then the insurgency and so on and so forth and fomenting a problem and then going in at some point and essentially just kind of taking over and creating a lot more discord?

And then the other question is, in the China, Russia, North Korea gambit, if China decides that they are going to kind of start choking off North Korea economically, Russia will no doubt, will no doubt fill the void. What should our action be at that time?

So those two questions, who is next and what action should we be contemplating?

Mr. CLARKE. Sir, I would say from—and again, I am a terrorism expert and I focus mostly on the Middle East, but from my broader reading, I would say I would be concerned about Moldova or one of the countries in the Baltics from a NATO purview.

Mr. CORNELL. Congressman, I think Russia is not finished in either Georgia or Ukraine, particularly in Georgia. The aim of the invasion in 2008 was not just to grab two pieces of land, Russia grabbed those pieces of land when it failed to achieve regime change, which Sergey Lavrov told Condoleezza Rice on the phone he wanted Saakashvili to go. Russia failed in achieving regime change.

Right now, Russia has, if you will, they have seen that because of a vacuum left by the United States in the Middle East they haven't really paid so much attention to the post-Soviet space in the past years. They have set their sights further to play an outsize role in areas of the Middle East and in Europe where the United States has normally been, so to speak, more influential.

At some point I wouldn't at all be surprised if they return to the South Caucasus either by targeting Georgia again or, as we saw examples of in April 2016, of fomenting a renewed war between Armenian and Azerbaijan that would enable them to move in to control the whole South Caucasus, which forms the access route for the United States and Europe into Central Asia and Afghanistan.

Mr. WILSON. Thank you, Congressman Perry. And actually Ranking Member Keating has some input for you about the Tsarnaev brothers.

Mr. KEATING. Just briefly, I don't want to take other members' times, but being familiar myself with that issue, Russia did indeed inform U.S. intelligence, including the FBI and CIA, of their concern. And they also asked our cooperation in giving them information because they perceived Tamerlan Tsarnaev as a threat and wanted the U.S. to give the information back. That is part of it. Thank you for allowing me to——

Mr. WILSON. Right. And thank you, Congressman Keating, for your very interesting input on that.

And we now proceed to Congressman Brendan Byrne of Pennsylvania.

Mr. BOYLE. Well, I am Brendan Boyle. Brendan Byrne was Governor of New Jersey. And Bradley Byrne is a colleague from Alabama.

Mr. WILSON. Well, it is a southern pronunciation.

Mr. BOYLE. Well, thank you.

And thank you to our witnesses for this rather interesting hearing for various reasons.

A few different points. The first is I had the opportunity this weekend to meet Yevgenia Albats, who is one of the few remaining truly independent journalists in Russia, and to hear from her firsthand about what it is like to try to be part of a free press, a rather dwindling free press in Russia, and it was eye opening; also sobering.

She is in the United States this week doing a fellowship at the University of Pennsylvania. If you have or anyone has had the opportunity to watch the excellent two-part series by "Frontline" called "Putin's Revenge," you will see her as well as a number of others that make quite clear Putin's intentions and actions.

The second point I want to raise is something that is always in the back of my mind any time we discuss Russia. In 1989, when the Berlin Wall fell, in East Germany, stationed there, was a KGB agent by the name of Vladimir Putin. He would go on to call the fall of the Soviet Union the single largest geopolitical catastrophe of the 20th century.

So any time, again, that we discuss Russia, we should keep that if not in the back of our mind, certainly the forefront, that that is the prism through which he views the U.S.-Russia relationship.

Now, I was going to ask Mr. Carpenter a question about something he pointed out in his written testimony. I will open that up to anyone who wants to comment. In his testimony he outlined quite well Russia's disregard for civilians in air strikes in Syria. In fact, according to Physicians for Human Rights, 90 percent—90 percent—of the attacks against hospitals and medical personnel were conducted by Russia and the Assad regime.

A, do you agree with this statistic from the Physicians for Human Rights? And second, how could anyone reasonably argue that Russia could possibly be an ally when it comes to counterterrorism when clearly their definition and our definition are quite different?

Mr. CLARKE. I would have to look at the data myself, but that is not really a surprising figure given what we know of the current situation in Syria, and I think just another reason to underscore why we should keep the Russians at arm's length in Syria and be very, very reticent of cooperating with Russia in the CT space.

Mr. CORNELL. Congressman, I have no doubt—no reason to doubt that statistic.

I think an important point when we talk about regimes abroad is there are a lot of authoritarian regimes. Now, there are authoritarian regimes that we can work with because that is the reality of the world. There are others that we should not work with.

And that brings back to my mind the brilliant essay by Jeane Kirkpatrick back in the late 1970s about dictatorships and double standards and I think we should apply a similar kind of thinking today.

If you look at various authoritarian regimes, what is their ideology? Are they fundamentally opposed to U.S. interests in the world? And are they fomenting anti-American opinions and values among their own population? Clearly, that is the case in Russia.

Whereas there are others, we can talk about many regimes that we work with that are also authoritarian, but they may allow their young people to form their own opinions and don't necessarily point in an anti-American direction or work to undermine the interests of the United States abroad.

I think in those cases we should work with authoritarian regimes because we may even improve the situation in those countries by working with them, rather than standing out and hectoring them and pointing fingers at them.

But when dealing with regimes that are so obviously domestic—just switch on RT or Sputnik and you find out the spewing out of anti-American propaganda and outright lies that is coming out of Russia, and they are doing that for a reason. And we have to keep that in mind.

Mr. BOYLE. I only have 30 seconds left, so I just want to switch very briefly to Hezbollah, because I recently had an amendment as part of legislation we passed that addressed Russian support for Hezbollah.

Russia has transferred weapons to Hezbollah, provided air cover through air strikes for Hezbollah foot soldiers, and protected Hezbollah-held territory with Russian air defense. Could any of you talk a little bit about Russia's motivations here for this strategic support for Hezbollah?

Mr. CLARKE. Sure, Congressman. I have written a lot about Lebanese Hezbollah, including Lebanese Hezbollah's gains in Syria and what we expect Hezbollah to look like post-Syria. It has received a lot of training. It has experienced a lot of on-the-ground tactical cooperation with the Russians; so working with a nation-state in support of the Assad regime.

And I think Russia's main interest is not having to deal with its own military, but actually working through a proxy or a cutout, and a highly capable one, I might add, in Lebanese Hezbollah, to fight against various jihadist groups on the ground, to include ISIS.

Mr. BOYLE. Thank you. I yield back.

Mr. WILSON. Thank you, Congressman Brendan Boyle.

And we now proceed to Congresswoman Lois Frankel of Florida.

Ms. FRANKEL. Thank you, Mr. Chairman. You got that right.

Mr. WILSON. As an old friend, of course.

Ms. FRANKEL. Thank you.

First of all, gentlemen, thank you all for being here. This has been a very interesting conversation or discussion today.

I am going to get back to the subject matter of this hearing, "Russia: Counterterrorism Partner or Fanning the Flames?" I want to start with two questions and maybe I will get a chance to ask another one.

The first is, I would like to know, what do you think are the implications, if any, of our President not recognizing or I think denying Russian interference with our election, despite the fact that our intelligence community unanimously has said there is interference? That is number one.

Number two, in my effort to be bipartisan in some sense, I would like you to give me your opinion of how a Russian involvement in the Iran agreement and, for example, removing chemical agents from Syria plays into your opinion that there should be no cooperation.

And then, I think, I guess, I do have a third question, which is could you explain what is the difference between, I think you said, we should communicate but not cooperate?

Mr. CORNELL. Congresswoman, with regard to the election issues, it is not my area of research. The only thing I would like to point out is I think everybody should understand that it is not about the support for a particular person or against a particular person, but an effort to undermine the legitimacy of the United

States and its political system both at home and abroad, and it is unfortunate that that becomes a partisan issue where it shouldn't be.

I think on the issues of Syria and Iran, when we talk about cooperation on counterterrorism, and several of us have said that we are skeptical of that notion, it doesn't mean we shouldn't have diplomatic relations with Russia. Counterterrorism cooperation is something much deeper. It is about intelligence sharing, actual joint operations, which would send exactly the wrong signal to Russia, particularly in view of their other activities.

Now, I think Iran and Syria fall into that category. I think, unfortunately, the previous administration opened the door, as was said by one of the Congressmen earlier, for Russia to take a position in the Middle East that it has not traditionally had. A colleague of mine calls Mr. Putin's regime the vacuum cleaner. Wherever they find a vacuum in international politics they fill that vacuum. And we have to make sure we don't create that type of vacuum for them.

On Iran, the only thing I would say, that yes, the Russians were partly cooperative in the Iranian nuclear agreement. They were also the force that helped bolster the Iranian nuclear program to begin with, beginning with all the Iranian nuclear reactors that they have built and all the material that they have sold to Iran.

Ms. FRANKEL. Did anyone else want to respond? If not, I have another question.

Mr. SARADZHYAN. The cases you pointed out are cases, in my view, that show that when it is in Russia's interest it cooperates with the U.S. on issues. It is in Russia's interest to prevent proliferation of nuclear weapons, and therefore it is in Russia's interest to reach an agreement with Iran on that issue if it puts constraints on Iran's ability to acquire nuclear weapons.

But if Russia were to choose between a diplomatic solution or a conflict with a nuclear weapon state, it would choose a diplomatic solution, even if it doesn't work. So Russia would not support the military operation against North Korea.

Ms. FRANKEL. Alright. Let me just go to my last question. One of my colleagues asked about, I think, what are the do's and the don't's of our communications or our interaction with Russia. I think Mr. Carpenter gave us some don't's. Does anybody have some do's?

Mr. CLARKE. Trust in God, but lock your car. I mean, I think we should be open minded with the relationship with Russia, but also very guarded. So, I mean, I know that sounds contradictory, but I don't think we should completely shut off the relationship, we should be highly skeptical, and as I noted earlier, I think very measured and very judicious.

Ms. FRANKEL. Alright. Thank you very much.

I yield back.

Mr. WILSON. Thank you, Congresswoman Frankel.

We now proceed to Congresswoman Norma Torres of California.

Mrs. TORRES. Thank you, Mr. Chairman.

Mr. Clarke, I have another saying: Pray for the best, but plan for the worst.

Overall, I think terrorism is a serious threat to our national security and we need partners, allies, to help us fight terror and protect our homeland. Fortunately, we have some great allies in Europe, in the Middle East, and in Latin America who share our interests and our common values and human decency.

Russia, on the other hand, does not share any of that. Russia certainly does not share our values or human decency.

I am sorry that Dr. Carpenter is no longer here, but I am hoping, Dr. Cornell, you can answer or you can try to address this issue.

Can you go into greater detail about corruption in the Russian Government? What is the impact of that corruption on the countries that Russia is currently involved in?

And I don't know if we speak about Russia in the same tone as we would speak about Putin since you have said that he is worth in the billions.

Mr. CORNELL. Congresswoman, I think there are two aspects. One of course, which is well known, I would only point to Karen Dawisha's book about Putin's kleptocracy, which details the rise of the system in detail.

I think the more important point, as we look at Russia's behavior on the international scene, is that Russia utilizes corruption as an instrument of statecraft. As I mentioned previously, Russia has its toolbox with everything from cyber, to military aggression, to economic sanctions, and everything in between, that they can use.

Corruption is one of those elements. And as I have done for many years, looked at Russian foreign policy, especially toward the Independent States of the former Soviet Union, I think we find very clearly that one of the reasons they are against the development of democratic institutions and accountability in those states is because they prefer to be able to deal, to build a sphere of influence, by having weak, corrupt semi-authoritarian governments in those countries, which are answerable to Russia because of the corrupt deals they have with Russia, rather than be answerable—accountable to their own people.

And I think you see this in Russia, the state of Russia. You see it also, obviously, in Russian corporations, Gazprom being the most important example, that are able to enter markets in a way that obviously American companies cannot do by the use of corruption, coercion, and intimidation.

Mrs. TORRES. So in other words, it is a Russian way of life.

Mr. CORNELL. I think it is Mr. Putin's regime's way of life. As you may have seen in the past couple of months, there are growing protests, public protests in Russia, by truck drivers and by other groups in society against the system in which they live. Because, as I mentioned previously, this is a regime, I wouldn't quite call it on the ropes, but this is a regime that is very vulnerable economically as a result of its overreliance on oil, as a result of its corruption and kleptocracy, which is based on stealing money rather than investing money into the society.

Mrs. TORRES. Which is why I really like to speak about the Russian people in a different way that we would speak about the Russian Government and their current leader.

Mr. CORNELL. I absolutely agree, Congresswoman. The only caveat I would say is that people are vulnerable to propaganda. Propaganda exists for a reason, which is that it works. And with the constant anti-American propaganda coming out of the Russian media, that unfortunately affects the opinion of the Russian people and will do so for years to many could.

Mrs. TORRES. Let me try to get another question.

Dr. Clarke, do you think that Russia's information war could expand to other parts of the world beyond Europe and the United States?

For example, one of our closest allies and neighbors here in the Western Hemisphere, Mexico, they have a pretty large election, a national election coming up next year. What do you think are the odds of Russia moving in to influence that election the way they influenced our election last year?

Mr. CLARKE. So I think—and my colleagues, Dr. Christopher Paul and Dr. Miriam Matthews, have a really great piece on this called "The Russian Firehose of Falsehood," that is a really excellent look at what Russia is doing in the information operation space.

And I think the odds are quite high simply because it has worked, and we have seen it work. And so when something works, the recipe is usually, yes, more of that. So I would not be surprised to see Russia meddling in other areas, as well, beyond its traditional sphere of influence.

Mrs. TORRES. Thank you. And I yield back.

Mr. WILSON. And thank you, Congressman Torres.

And now Congressman Brad Sherman of California, who was my colleague yesterday at a conference here in Washington, a soul mate.

Mr. SHERMAN. Thank you.

I would point out that, especially after the fall of the Soviet Union, the U.S. gratuitously took anti-Russian positions. Wherever there was a dispute over territorial integrity versus self-determination, in each case we came out against the Russian position, whether that be Kosovo or northern Kosovo or the border regions of Croatia, et cetera.

That being said, I don't think any of us is surprised. We have to do business with Russia. But we shouldn't be fooled. And don't only lock your car, Dr. Clarke, get an alarm, park under the light, et cetera.

The Muslim world is in a three-way civil war between moderate Sunnis, extremist Brotherhood-influenced Sunnis, and a Shiite alliance based in Tehran. You have got over 20 million mostly Sunni Muslims in Russia, yet Russia has decided to take the Shiite position.

Is there any effort by Russia's over 20 million Sunni Muslims to get their country to be less accommodating to the Shiites and more accommodating to the Sunnis?

Mr. CORNELL. Congressman, I think there are growing frustrations among Russia's Sunni Muslim population on this issue. I think, however, that most of these people—and actually most of the people in Russia's neighborhood continue to be dominated by Russian-controlled media, state-controlled media, which means that they are not—I don't think they fully have the same information space as we do, to put it mildly.

Mr. SHERMAN. Well, they know that the Russian Government is supporting the Alawites in Syria. They know that the Russian Government is friendly toward Tehran. They know there is a Shiite-Sunni conflict. Is this fine with the imams among the Tatars and Chechnyans and others?

Mr. CORNELL. Congressman, I think that is one of the reasons why so many young people of Muslim origin in Russia are being recruited into jihadi groups.

I would also point out that we very often talk about Central Asia as a locus of radicalization. In fact, all of that radicalization takes place outside of Central Asia. Over 85 percent of the Central Asian recruits into ISIS and other jihadi groups in Syria and Iraq have been radicalized while being labor migrants in Russia, not in their home countries, and that points to a serious problem there.

Mr. SHERMAN. I mean, there was a man who came from Uzbekistan to the United States and he radicalized here as far as we can tell.

Mr. CORNELL. Yes, yes.

Mr. SHERMAN. And is Russia more friendly with the Shiites because they don't pose a radicalization threat? It would be hard for Iran to emerge as a leader of Sunni Muslims in Russia or anywhere in their near abroad. Have they intentionally picked the side that has the least appeal for their own Muslims?

Mr. CORNELL. Sir, that may be a contributing factor. I think the main factor is that Iran has been a strategic partner for Russia because of its posture against the United States in the Middle East, and because they early on in the 1990s joined forces in preventing the growth of U.S. influence in the neighborhood of Russia, especially in Central Asian and the Caucasus, Iran being in the south of the Caspian Sea, Russia in the north, trying to thwart U.S. influence in that region between them.

It is a purely geopolitical interest that predates the real big conflict between Sunnis and Shias.

Mr. CLARKE. I would say ditto for Syria, a traditional long-standing Cold War ally, as well, and long-time purchaser of Russian weapons.

Mr. SHERMAN. And is our broadcasting to the Russian people effective on these issues?

Dr. Cornell.

Mr. CORNELL. Sir, I just call the attention to studies by the U.S. Government itself that have found foreign broadcasting to be very subpar. I think there is a serious problem in the efforts by the United States to reach out to communities that are potentially interested in hearing the American viewpoint on things in the world.

Mr. SHERMAN. Is this because our technology doesn't get the message onto their device, whether it be computer or radio, or because our message is lame, or just because we are not believed?

Mr. CORNELL. I think it is the two first ones. I think the message needs serious improvement. I think also, if we look at the staffing of the radios and TV stations that we operate, they are heavily operated by people who are exiles from their own countries who have lost touch with their countries many years ago. I think there are many aspects to be looked at there.

Mr. SHERMAN. And are we as effective on the Internet as we are—
I mean, there is a tendency for the government to lag behind
technology. Are we doing as much as we should on the Internet as
opposed to radio broadcasting, the technology of the 1970s, where
we at least have a bureaucracy that is into that? What about the
Internet?

Mr. CLARKE. So, I think this falls into the general sphere and extends to our areas to counter violent extremism or prevent terrorism writ large. We are very good at the kinetic aspects of CT,
tanks, guns, bombs. We have for too long put off countering the
narrative as the softer side of counterterrorism and we have seen
with the current conflict with the Islamic State that we have got
a long way to go.

Mr. SHERMAN. My time has expired. I thank the chairman for
staying late and——

Mr. WILSON. And thank you, Mr. Sherman.

I want to thank Ranking Member Keating, all of our witnesses
today, thank you for being here, and the professional staff of the
Foreign Affairs Committee. The United States is fortunate to have
such dedicated personnel.

Thank you very much, and we are adjourned.

[Whereupon, at 4:20 p.m., the subcommittees were adjourned.]

APPENDIX

MATERIAL SUBMITTED FOR THE RECORD

JOINT SUBCOMMITTEE HEARING NOTICE
COMMITTEE ON FOREIGN AFFAIRS
U.S. HOUSE OF REPRESENTATIVES
WASHINGTON, DC 20515-6128

Subcommittee on Terrorism, Nonproliferation, and Trade
Ted Poe (R-TX), Chairman

Subcommittee on Europe, Eurasia, and Emerging Threats
Dana Rohrabacher (R-CA), Chairman

TO: MEMBERS OF THE COMMITTEE ON FOREIGN AFFAIRS

You are respectfully requested to attend an OPEN hearing of the Committee on Foreign Affairs, to be held jointly by the Subcommittee on Terrorism, Nonproliferation, and Trade and the Subcommittee on Europe, Eurasia, and Emerging Threats in Room 2172 of the Rayburn House Office Building (and available live on the Committee website at http://www.ForeignAffairs.house.gov):

DATE: Tuesday, November 7, 2017

TIME: 2:00 p.m.

SUBJECT: Russia: Counterterrorism Partner or Fanning the Flames?

WITNESSES: Colin P. Clarke, Ph.D.
Political Scientist
RAND Corporation

Svante Cornell, Ph.D.
Senior Fellow for Eurasia
Director of the Central Asia-Caucasus Institute
American Foreign Policy Council

Mr. Simon Saradzhyan
Director of the Russia Matters Project
Assistant Director of U.S.-Russia Initiative to Prevent Nuclear Terrorism
Belfer Center for Science and International Affairs
Harvard Kennedy School

Michael Carpenter, Ph.D.
Nonresident Senior Fellow
Dinu Patriciu Eurasia Center
Atlantic Council
Senior Director of the Biden Center for Diplomacy and Global Engagement
University of Pennsylvania

By Direction of the Chairman

COMMITTEE ON FOREIGN AFFAIRS

MINUTES OF SUBCOMMITTEE ON _Terrorism, Nonproliferation, and Trade & Europe, Eurasia, and Emerging Threats_ HEARING

Day____*Tuesday*____Date____*11/07/2017*____Room____2172____

Starting Time ____*2:16pm*____ Ending Time ____*4:20pm*____

Recesses |____| (____to ____) (____to ____) (____to ____) (____to ____) (____to ____) (____to ____)

Presiding Member(s)

Representative Poe, Representative Wilson, Representative Perry

Check all of the following that apply:

Open Session ☑
Executive (closed) Session ☐
Televised ☐

Electronically Recorded (taped) ☑
Stenographic Record ☑

TITLE OF HEARING:

"Russia: Counterterrorism Partner or Fanning the Flames?"

SUBCOMMITTEE MEMBERS PRESENT:

Rep. Poe, Keating, Rohrabacher, Meeks, Wilson, Sherman, Cook, Sires, Perry, Cicilline, Zeldin, Frankel, Mast, Kelly, Rooney, Boyle, Fitzpatrick, Titus, Torres, Schneider

NON-SUBCOMMITTEE MEMBERS PRESENT: *(Mark with an * if they are not members of full committee.)*

Rep. Donovan

HEARING WITNESSES: Same as meeting notice attached? Yes ☑ No ☐
(If "no", please list below and include title, agency, department, or organization.)

STATEMENTS FOR THE RECORD: *(List any statements submitted for the record.)*

SFR submitted by Rohrabacher

TIME SCHEDULED TO RECONVENE __________
or
TIME ADJOURNED ____*4:20pm*____

Subcommittee Staff Associate

Rep. Dana Rohrabacher Opening Statement

TNT/EE&ET Joint Subcommittee Hearing, "Russia: Counterterrorism Partner or Fanning the Flames?"

November 7, 2017

Chairman Poe, thank you for initiating today's hearing and I am happy to be part of what I think will be an important discussion. In my Subcommittee, I held a hearing on a similar topic just over two years ago. Since then, we have a new President in the White House who is genuinely interested seeing if relations with Russia can be improved. I believe that this is a positive development for both our countries.

It is significant that today is the 100 year anniversary of the Bolshevik revolution, a date which reminds us of the dark and bloody Soviet history. Although there are those who would treat Russia today as if it were still the Soviet Union, that period of time is now behind us. Although the flaws of the current Russian government are evident, it behooves us to recognize the change that has taken place. When Russia was the Soviet Union, it was our primary enemy. Now, that enemy is radical Islamic terrorism. And Islamic terrorism threatens Russia as well; thus, there are opportunities for cooperation.

The fight against violent, radical Islam is the major challenge of our time. As we saw last week in the streets of Manhattan, the threat of radical Islam is pervasive. Radicalized Muslims have slaughtered innocents not just in the Middle East but in Europe, and yes, in Russia. These terrorists have declared war on the modern, civilized world. The future of America, Russia and, yes, western civilization depends on the defeat of this enemy, just as we defeated Nazism and communism.

In the aftermath of the Boston Bombing, in May of 2013, I led a Congressional Delegation to Russia. We met with Russian government and intelligence officials and discussed the threat of terrorism and how our governments could potentially cooperate. Clearly many things have gotten in the way of our closer cooperation, but it would be a profound mistake to cease efforts to find common ground and mutually-beneficial cooperation.

It's no secret that I've been disappointed by the downward spiral of the US-Russia relationship and the downsizing of our mutual diplomatic missions. Yet, despite that drag, our governments have still managed admirable levels of cooperation in some areas, such as the international space station. And, in a few days, President Trump will be meeting with President Putin to discuss, among other things, possible efforts to deal with the threat of a North Korea with nuclear weapons and long-range missiles. This type of possible cooperation to achieve a positive mutually-beneficial goal has been undermined by ten years of hostility.

I thank the witnesses for their time and effort and look forward to hearing each of your testimonies.